DELOREAN
TIME MACHINE

OWNERS' WORKSHOP MANUAL

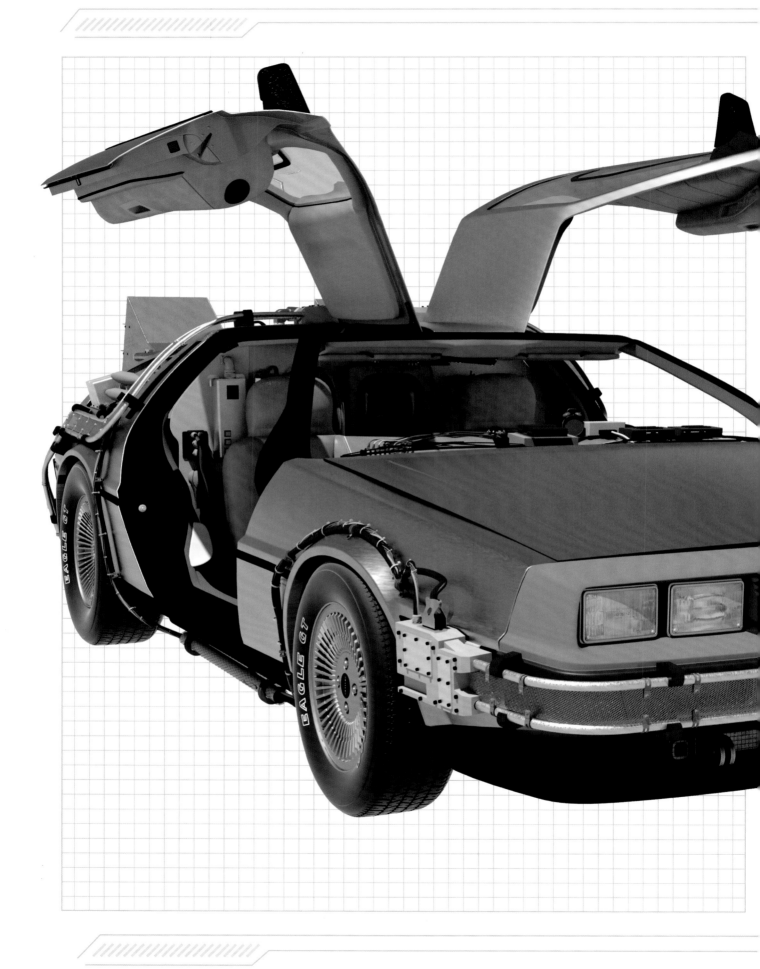

BACK TO THE FUTURE™

DELOREAN TIME MACHINE

OWNERS' WORKSHOP MANUAL

BOB GALE and **JOE WALSER**
Illustrations by **JOE WALSER**
Introduction by **DOCTOR EMMETT L. BROWN**

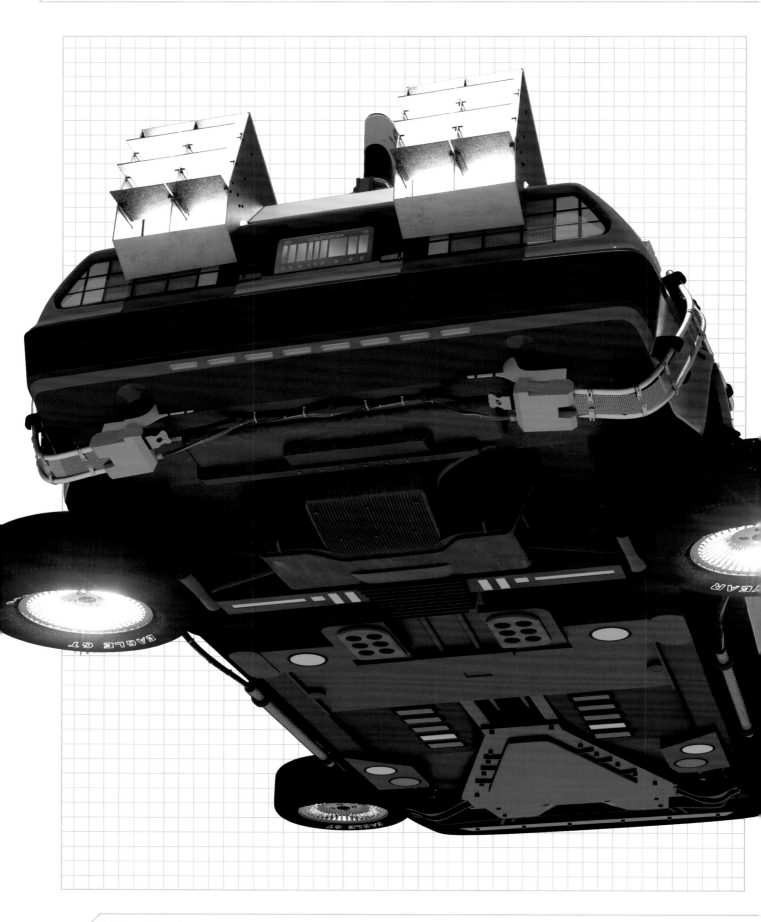

CONTENTS

INTRODUCTION

MY NAME IS Doctor Emmett Lathrop Brown, physicist and inventor. I am, of course, stating the obvious because you, dear reader, are already aware of that fact, as it has been previously revealed on the title page. But this is an introduction, so, in the interest of taking the definition of that word literally, I believe it appropriate to formally introduce myself. Now that task has been completed.

This book is my attempt to recount the creation and development of various technical aspects of my greatest invention, the flux capacitor, which led to my ultimate achievement: the DeLorean Time Machine. This technology has never been patented, but I write this in the interest of posterity and to dispel any alternate versions of the history of these inventions. And yet, I have learned that history is malleable, with infinite variations, so no one can

(nor should) say with certainty that a particular version of history is "correct." Thus, what follows is essentially correct in the timeline in which I have written it, although it may not be completely accurate in the timeline in which it is being published, nor in the one in which you are reading it.

The volume includes excerpts from my personal journals and papers, as well as some photographs and other images created exclusively for this publication. Some key information has been redacted for security and other reasons. Most importantly, the actual practical and scientific methodology of the workings of the flux capacitor (which is what makes time travel possible) and time circuitry is not included, nor have I ever written it down. As I inherently understood, and which was subsequently demonstrated to me in more ways than one,

time travel is a dangerous thing, even more dangerous than the secrets of atomic energy. Ever since the development of atomic weapons in our government's Manhattan Project in Los Alamos, New Mexico (of which I was a part) and the use of those atomic weapons in Japan in 1945, the pros and cons of nuclear energy have been debated. Would the world have been a better place had we not developed nuclear weapons? Or was their invention inevitable once Albert Einstein published his equations demonstrating that nuclear weapons were feasible? Personally, I subscribe to the latter view, since history has shown us that the Nazis were working to develop such weapons simultaneously with our American efforts.

It is a fact that all inventors want to prove that their inventions are viable, if for no other reason than self-gratification, particularly after expending copious amounts of time and money. Simply put, we want to prove "it works!" It was therefore no surprise that an atomic weapon, once invented, would be used. So too, a time machine, once invented, would also be used. And I have used mine. I believe this use was largely for the sake of science, and certainly not for personal gain (although that too can be debated). But in all the Universe, there is one law that cannot be violated: The Law of Unintended Consequences. The unintended consequences of time travel are infinite, as I discovered in my own adventures. It requires little imagination to postulate the myriad ways

in which time travel could be misused. Hence secrecy in this regard is absolutely necessary. In fact, a convincing case can be made that <u>any</u> use of time travel constitutes a misuse, and I could argue that position with clarity and passion. So to that offense, I plead guilty.

Note that had I filed a patent on the flux capacitor, it would have required the submittal of key information to the United States Patent Office. It is not hard to imagine that another capable inventor could discover my documents and recreate my invention, and then use time travel to file his own patent for my own invention prior to my filing. The extrapolation of that concept boggles the mind.

But I digress. There is no patent, nor (if I can help it) will there ever be one. The critical information is inside my brain, never to be revealed. Some of the information and equations in this book are false, as additional insurance to protect the secrets of time travel from falling into the wrong hands.

But let us no longer focus on the dark side of time travel. There is much joy in discovery and invention, and it is that joy I wish to share. Thank you for your indulgence.

Respectfully submitted,

Emmett L. Brown

FROM AN UNDISCLOSED TIME AND PLACE IN THE SPACE-TIME CONTINUUM

DOC BROWN'S JOURNALS
1946–1985

March 6, 1946

Time travel via a time machine. The idea has fascinated me ever since I read H. G. Wells's novel. Is it possible? No matter what I do, my mind constantly returns to that conundrum. It is for this reason that I collect clocks—each a time machine in itself.

   With the end of the war, there are a lot of unemployed physicists. Unfortunately, General Leslie Groves, the overseer of the Manhattan Project, did not write letters of recommendation for any of us, which I suppose is a necessary by-product of involvement in a top-secret project. Nevertheless, I hope to find some sort of real-world employment, as I fear that becoming a university professor would eventually lead to mental atrophy. As much as I admire Albert Einstein, I am doubtful that his situation at Princeton will result in any more breakthroughs.

May 14, 1946

I have been hired by King Class Technologies to work on a classified project. They have also hired ███████ and ██████, and I believe it was the latter who recommended me. I am hopeful that the camaraderie and exchange of ideas we experienced in Los Alamos will continue in this new environment in California.

Sept. 1945, from left, Kenneth Bainbridge, Joseph Hoffmann, J. Robert Oppenheimer, Louis Hempelmann, Victor Weisskopf, me, Robert Bacher, Richard Dodson.

May 20, 1946

As I prepare for my new endeavor, I fondly recall many theoretical discussions about time travel with some of the other physicists in New Mexico. Although many were skeptical of the concept, several, such as Dr. John Barber and Professor Derek Fridolfs, had observations and ideas that remain encouraging. I look forward to exploring these concepts in my spare time after work, and hope to find some like-minded colleagues.

June 17, 1946

As I begin my third week here, I find myself in a stifling environment. My supervisor knows little of physics and even less about how to encourage creative thinking. I never imagined I would have a job that required me to punch a clock or wear a tie.

July 12, 1946

I wish I could afford to quit this job, but I need the money. Meanwhile, I am quietly searching for other employment.

KING CLASS TECHNOLOGIES, INC.

NOTICE OF TERMINATION OF EMPLOYMEN

Effective __6__ ☐ a.m., ☒ p.m., on _____5/27/1949_____, your empl will be terminated on Project No. _____6405_____

Cause of termination: ....Dress code violations.....
Report: ...After receiving two reprimands for this offense, Dr. Brown once again wore a Hawaiian shirt under his lab coat. Such deviation from our high standards will not be tolerated at this company.........

Name:
Address:
City:

October 22, 1949

I have found working as an appliance repairman to be amazingly liberating. It has taught me a practical craft, and I have learned a great deal about 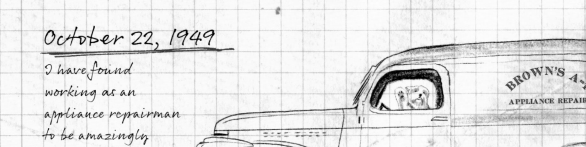 the inner workings of refrigerators, stoves, air conditioners, and televisions. I have even made improvements to some of my clients' devices, ensuring they will last far beyond their rated lives. Most importantly, the job allows me time to do mental thought experiments on new inventions. And, I have acquired a canine companion from the local dog shelter, whom I have named Copernicus.

August 10, 1950

Last night, my mother phoned to inform me that my father had died. They had lived apart for over a decade and had had only minimal communication since their separation, so she was more philosophical than emotional. This describes my own state as well, given my basically perfunctory conversations with him after graduating college. Father (as he never allowed me to call him "Dad") was a cold man, which may have had its advantages in dispensing justice, but did not endear him to many, myself included. On the other hand, had he been a better, warmer parent, perhaps I would not have been so resolute about defying his wishes by turning my energies to science rather than following in his footsteps. I do believe in his own way he took pride in the fact that I participated in the Manhattan Project and helped win the war. And I will certainly attend the funeral.

November 16, 1950

When my father died in August, his fortune came to me. Due to his estrangement from my mother, she was left only a token amount. With probate now closed, there should be an ample amount for me to finance my experiments. Meanwhile, I have been enjoying his 1949 Packard convertible, truly a fine automobile.

January 11, 1951

My return to Hill Valley so many years after high school was, simply put, anti-climactic. Although I had many acquaintances, I had no real friends anymore, as the several classmates who had shared my love of science had also left — and who could blame them? We had all been disparaged as eggheads. But I determined this to be advantageous to my plans. Without any social pressures, I would be free to pursue my experiments in solitude, without interruption. To further ensure my privacy, I dropped hints about my current work that were designed to protect my property, including a letter to the Editor of the local paper.

Emmett Brown, Son of the Late Judge Erhardt Brown, Returns to Hill Valley

Dr. Emmett Brown, the Hill Valley physicist who worked on the Manhattan Project, has returned to Hill Valley after the death of his father, Judge Erhardt Brown, in August. Brown, a former professor at his alma mater, Cal Tech, grew up in Hill Valley and graduated Hill Valley High School in 1933. He has moved into the Riverside Drive home of his late parent where he said he plans to carry out research and conduct experi-

Letters to the Editor

Dear Editor,

I am writing to report strange goings-on at 1640 Riverside Drive. I have come to understand that its resident, Emmett Brown, is a scientist who worked on the Manhattan Project and helped develop the atomic bomb. While walking my dog, I have seen flickering lights and have heard strange sounds coming from the house. As of last week, my dog no longer will go near that property. I have heard rumors that several scientists are developing a death ray for the government, and that might be the reason. Regardless, I will be staying away from the 1600 block of Riverside Drive for the foreseeable future, and I urge my neighbors to do the same.

Sincerely,
Herbert George

September 30, 1954

Time travel will require the release of a dynamic burst of energy. In normal circuitry, a sudden electrical release would be facilitated via an aluminum or tantalum capacitor. But the amount of energy theoretically necessary is beyond the specifications of any existing capacitor. A new design will be required...

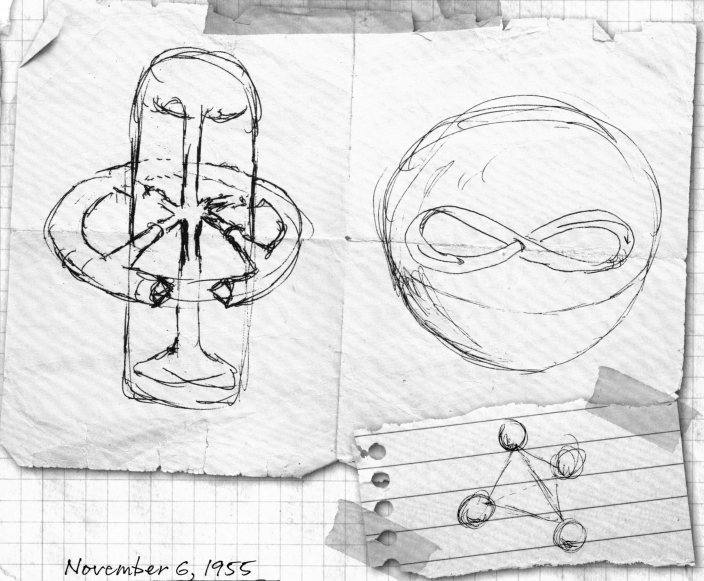

November 6, 1955

There have been myriad scientific breakthroughs that occurred as a result of fortuitous flukes. Such a lucky accident befell me yesterday. I was standing on the edge of my toilet, hanging a clock. The porcelain was wet, I slipped, hit my head on the sink, and lost consciousness. When I regained cognizance, the blunt force trauma resulted in my having a vision—a picture in my head—which I immediately sketched on the first medium I could find: a paper napkin. I believe it to be the answer I've been searching for: the flux capacitor.

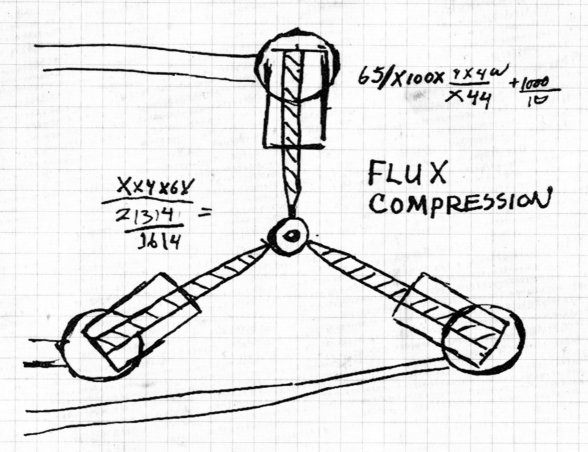

$$\frac{X \times Y \times 6Y}{21314} = \frac{1614}{}$$

$$65/X100X \frac{Y \times 4W}{X44} + \frac{1000}{10}$$

FLUX COMPRESSION

January 29, 1956

At some future date, the improvement in transistor technology should make it possible to build a version of the flux capacitor that will be the size of a breadbox. But until I am able to prove its viability to myself, I must construct a much larger version using tried-and-true vacuum tubes, particularly for the time circuitry.

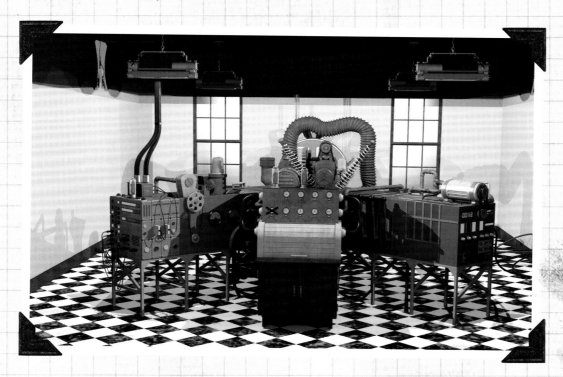

March 11, 1956

Given the size of the device and associated components, my experiments will focus on sending a small object several moments into the future. It must be this way because only time travel into the future is experimentally demonstrable. For example, if I could send an apple 10 seconds into the future, to my perception, it would "disappear" from the moment of time travel, and I would catch up with it ten seconds later, causing it to "reappear" to my senses. The reality would be that the apple "skipped over" those 10 seconds. But I don't know about time travel into the past. If I attempted to send the same apple 10 seconds into the past, how would I know if I succeeded? And wouldn't it have already happened? And wouldn't that be a paradox? There is much danger inherent in such experimentation.

May 3, 1956

Today's experiment was unsuccessful. I only succeeded in blowing out all of the fuses in the electrical panel and terrorizing poor Copernicus in the process who promptly retreated to his little dog house...

Inserting pennies to replace the burned out fuses permits me to power my house, but not the flux capacitor. I must therefore construct a replacement electrical panel that will handle a much higher load...

CALIFORNIA STANDARD POLICY

Expires	August 16, 1957
Property	House
Previous Amount . . .	$ 800,000
Actual Amunt . . .	$ 4,000,000

No. 25001549

THE
FAR WEST INSURANCE
FIRE INSURANCE COMPANY
HILL VALLEY.

HERBERT E KING, AGENT,
HILL VALLEY, CALIFORNIA

BANTON ELECTRIC
HARDWARE AND ELECTRONICS

Date ___May___ 1956

Sold to _Ernett Brown_

	Am't For'd			
	By Produce			
	Balance			
48 Amp Plug Fuse			$.20	$9.60
48 Wire Connector			$.10	$4.80
48 Wire Stripper and Cutter			$1.00	$48.00

t is important that the written portions of all policies
ing the same property read exactly alike. If they do not they
d be made uniform at once.

October 18, 1956

Preliminary tests show that my new panel will allow me to utilize four times more electrical power than the one I burned out. However, I am not sure if that will be enough...

My latest experiment caused an aptly named brownout in the neighborhood. My neighbors are not amused. Neither was the man from Hill Valley Power and Light.

SAN DIEGO, _May 2, 1957_

Dr. Brown
Bought of

AXJ
INDUSTRIAL SUPPLY

W. RANDOLPH ST.

Phones Haymarket 2678
Monroe 9524

SCG Model 3 Power Transformer	1	23.000

TWR PARTS AND ENGINEERING

DATE _May 21, 1957_

SOLD TO _Emmett Brown_

BTX 350-D Generator	$18.275
Sempra Coil Assembly-3	$1.050
GX-30 Industrial Grade Cable - insulated -100 feet	$2.400

W. RA

S
Tra

BS   enging   4   3.996

Letters to the Editor

Dear Editor,

I am writing to report strange goings-on at 1640 Riverside Drive. I have come to understand that its resident, Emmett Brown, is a scientist who worked on the Manhattan Project and helped develop the atomic bomb. While walking my dog, I have seen flickering lights and have heard strange sounds coming from the house. As of last week, my dog no longer will go near that property. I have heard rumors that several scientists are developing a death ray for the government,

November 15, 1956

I have calculated that the amount of electricity I require will necessitate my own source of power. Therefore, I must procure or build my own generator. It will not be inexpensive.

December 9, 1956

I purchased a dynamo from a mothballed cruise ship. Transporting it here will be challenging and expensive, but still more cost-effective than building my own.

March 29, 1957

Refurbishing this equipment is becoming a longer and more costly process than I estimated...

September 21, 1957

Expenses are becoming a problem.

March 4, 1958

I am proud to state that I have at last restored the dynamo to working order. However, to ensure its operation, it may be necessary to procure industrial-grade gasoline storage tanks on the scale of those used underground at service stations.

May 25, 1959

A breakthrough of sorts, yesterday. I believe I successfully sent a 1/16" metal screw two seconds into the future! On the other hand, I may have simply dropped it.

September 14, 1960

I attended the 6:45 showing of George Pal's production of H.G. Wells' "The Time Machine" at the Essex Theater. It was an excellent film, and brought to mind aspects of the novel that I had forgotten.

ESSEX THEATER
Good Date Sold Only
ADULT AUD'M 75 CENTS
ADMIT ONE
ADULT AUD'M 75 CENTS
480558

Time travel into the future is something we all do, every day, one second at a time. On a purely theoretical level, then, time travel into the future is pointless unless one can travel back to one's starting point, just as H.G. Wells concluded. Therefore, I must redouble my efforts toward traveling backward in time.

My own theoretical equations demonstrate that time travel into the past can go no further back than to the time of the first activation of the time machine. The only way to go further is if the machine itself can travel with the time traveler. Again, I tip my hat to the vision of H.G. Wells. (Perhaps he himself was a time traveler!)

May 26, 1961

I applaud President Kennedy's announcement yesterday about a national goal of landing a man on the moon before the decade is out. In addition to the glory of such an accomplishment, the research and development required to achieve this goal will lead to technological breakthroughs that will aid humanity on all levels, and expand our scientific horizons...

October 23, 1962

I barely slept last night. President Kennedy announced that the Soviet Union had placed nuclear missiles in Cuba and that America would not tolerate this. Are we on the brink of World War III? And if so, will it be my duty to take part in the war effort? Tense times. Even Copernicus was on edge, although this was undoubtedly a result of him being tuned into my own distress and unease.

LAUNCH STANDS

17 MISSILE ERECTORS

October 24, 1962

I was surprised to have General Leslie Groves call on me today. Given the Cuban Missile Crisis, I would have expected his attention to be solely focused on that emergency. I was doubly impressed that he remembered my speculations about time travel when we were at Los Alamos together, particularly given my junior status on the project. And this was the reason for his visit: The government is considering a "Manhattan Project" for time travel, to be managed by Colonel Edward Lomax, who accompanied Groves to my home. Groves wanted to know if I had made any progress, specifically noting that if a time traveler could be sent on a mission to Cuba to prevent the ascent of Fidel Castro and the Communist regime, there would be no current missile crisis, and the world would be a safer place. Groves was receptive to the research I presented, including a crude experiment involving two candles, one of which I sent 90 seconds into the future, the proof shown by the fact that it had barely melted compared to the control candle. However, Lomax was less than impressed, given that the demonstration did not indicate that time travel to the past was even possible. Copernicus took an immediate dislike to Lomax, and I can't dismiss his instincts. Still, the prospect of getting nearly unlimited funding from the government is enticing, and the project could help make the world a safer place. It would certainly be liberating to focus solely on the science and technology without concern for financing. And the idea that I could have a team of physicists and technicians working under me is, to quote Shakespeare, "a consummation devoutly to be wished." I expect to hear from them both again in the next week or two.

October 25, 1962

Great Scott, what was I thinking?? I just woke up from a vivid and powerful nightmare, involving Nazis, the Red Army, Roman Legions and Conquistadors, all with time machines and atomic weapons — a clear reminder of what I already knew: allowing the military or any government the ability to utilize time travel is dangerous and irresponsible. Even given the best intentions, it would be inevitable that the secrets and technology would be stolen by others with baser motivations, as evidenced by the theft of America's nuclear secrets. My immediate mission now is to convince General Groves and Colonel Lomax <u>not</u> to finance my experiments nor to pay my theories any heed. As always, encouraging the perception of myself as a "crackpot inventor" is my best guarantee for safety, solitude, and discouragement of outside interference. I am already developing an idea...

BROWN MANSION DESTROYED

Fire Engulfs Hill Valley Landmark, Burned to the Ground

Research experiment apparently went awry. Crackpot inventor says his theories were wrong.

Shortly after 10 p.m. last night, flames suddenly enveloped the Riverside Drive home of Dr. Emmett L. Brown, burning the structure to the ground. Hill Valley Fire Department trucks were too late to save the house, although the ga- minor burns and told authorities that he believed the fire was accidentally instigated by an electrical overload in a relay switch that was triggered during one of his experiments. The house was built in 1910 by architects Greene & Greene un-

November 18, 1962

I am thankful that my fire insurance was paid up and will cover the damages.

November 24, 1962

I have reconfigured my garage workshop area to accommodate a cot. The living quarters will not be as spacious as what I'd become accustomed to, but will still be superior to the arrangements at Los Alamos.

June 15, 1963

The problems of a self-contained time machine may be best solved by installing the time circuitry into an automobile, as it would afford the greatest mobility in a contained space. This would require that I invent some sort of temporal field displacement device which would create a bubble around the vehicle that would safely transport it and its occupant through the space-time continuum. I believe I know how to construct such a device. However, the amount of electrical energy to accomplish such a task would exceed one gigawatt, a power requirement not easily attainable. For the time being, I shall relegate this problem to the back burner, as further experimentation is required to complete the time circuitry.

I am concerned that I will soon run short of funds...

November 28, 1963

The assassination of President Kennedy has depressed me for a week. And I can't help wondering, if I had a functional time machine, could I have prevented it? Or <u>should</u> I have prevented it? Questions with no answers — at least not until I actually have a functional time machine. I must refocus my efforts and put my mind to accomplishing my task.

September 9, 1964

I am still mourning the passing of my faithful companion, Copernicus. No one could have had a better friend, and I miss him daily. It is unfortunate that the canine life span is not longer, but I am grateful to have had almost 15 years of joy with him. Although he can never be replaced, I know there are other abandoned dogs who need good homes and, because the thought of being without a pup is now simply incomprehensible, I shall endeavor to rescue one of them in the coming days.

September 23, 1964

Today I welcomed a new addition to the family. I have named him "Edison" as I know he will be a shining light in my life.

April 30, 1965

The money from the sale of the estate should provide the financing I need for my continued work. And the heavy construction that will inevitably ensue will mask the sounds of my own work.

June 1, 1968

Only a nuclear reactor would be capable of generating a full gigawatt of electricity...

February 21, 1975

Scientific advancement in nuclear power plants proceeds at a snail's pace, although General Electric's new S6G reactor for submarines promises great things for the future. It seems that what I want to do requires technology that is not yet feasible, either scientifically or economically. Will I have to wait? I may need to educate myself...

March 12, 1979

Mrs. Marcuse, who runs the shelter, said that sheepdogs were among the most intelligent breeds, so I have named my new pup "Einstein."

September 19, 1980

I have been commuting to Stanford to take a refresher class in nuclear physics. My status allows me access to their outstanding library, and I have been absorbing information from myriad scientific journals. There is good news and bad news. The good news is that I am convinced that it's possible to generate the electricity I need by use of a small plutonium-powered reactor. The bad news is that I have no idea how I could possibly procure any plutonium.

September 30, 1980

A car made of stainless steel! Such a vehicle could solve the flux dispersal problem. I hope it doesn't turn out to be an automotive pipe dream...

November 6, 1980

After class today, Achmed, a Libyan exchange student (at least I think he said he was Libyan), asked me if I'd heard about the Princeton student who claimed to have built a nuclear bomb. I told him I had but, given my own knowledge and experiences, it was unlikely such a homemade device would be functional. It was strange because he seemed to know I had worked on the Manhattan Project, which is not something I advertise. He said he might get in touch with me later, but why, I have no idea...

October 2, 1982

Today, surprisingly, I acquired a young assistant, one Martin McFly, aged 14. He was clever enough to defeat my alarm system algorithms, is curious, and fearless, and was honest in admitting that he had broken into my lab to procure some tubes for his guitar amplifier, because I had indeed bought up the entire local supply. Resourcefulness and forthrightness! So I did the only logical thing I could think of: I offered him a job, along with the tubes he wanted. He accepted both offers. His youthful inquisitiveness is refreshing and invigorating. And he passed the "Einstein test"— the dog simply loves him. I have a good feeling about the lad, and feel confident I can trust him.

October 16, 1982

Marty has been of immense help in recent days. He is able to procure items without anyone suspecting they are for me. And when his curiosity rises, he is satisfied to be told "all your questions will be answered." I look forward to the day when they will.

October 23, 1982

To protect both myself and young Marty, it will be necessary for me to secure a second workshop to use for my nuclear experiments, about which Marty must never know. That is, until the time is right.

REAL ESTATE PURCHASE AND SALE A...

IN WITNESS THEREOF, the parties hereto ha... this agreement for the following property as of t... below written.

Pre-Fab Steel Garage, 20 x 40 x 9, 2240 Industrial Drive, $23,999

"SELLER"

ARMSTRONG REALTY

Name: Joe Wilson
Title: Realtor

Date: November 11, 1982

November 19, 1982

This new work space is perfect. The fact that it was once a garage makes it even better, as I can use it for my automotive work...

December 10, 1983

Since I will have to reconfigure much of the vehicle, it makes little economic sense to buy a new car. Therefore, I will investigate the purchase of a used DeLorean, assuming I can find one at an acceptable price.

February 3, 1984

I headed over to the car dealer and, after a quick inspection, paid cash for the DeLorean right on the spot. VIN# SCEDT26T8BD005261 rolled off the Belfast assembly line in October 1981, with a grooved hood, a gray interior, a five-speed manual transmission, and a destiny: to become the DeLorean Time Machine!

AUTOMOBILES

1981 DELOREAN, 30,000 miles, MT, very good condition. $13K. Come on down, see Rudy Russo – New Deal Used Cars, Valley Road at the freeway

No wonder sales of the car did not meet expectations. The vehicle is seriously underpowered. Apparently the engineers didn't consider the cumulative weight of stainless steel compared to conventional auto body steel when they selected the Peugeot-Renault-Volvo 130 horsepower 6-cylinder engine. And given the additional weight of the nuclear reactor I must install, a complete engine rebuild will be necessary.

March 14, 1984

I decided to replace the stock V6 engine with a Porsche 928 V8. Given the vehicle's unique power requirements, I also upgraded the alternator/generator, and created a regenerative braking system while using the rotation of the wheels to rapid charge some of the systems, thereby keeping them independent from each other and less likely to suffer a catastrophic power failure.

April 7, 1984

I feel bad keeping secrets from Marty about the vehicle and my intentions for it. Thankfully, Marty has gotten to know me well enough that he accepts my reticence about my current project. He compared my behavior to his own creative endeavors. "I get it, Doc," he said. "It's like when I'm working on a new song, I don't want anyone to hear it until I think it's absolutely ready." Thankfully, he hasn't inquired about the various head bruises I've sustained getting in and out of the car.

August 22, 1984

For testing, it will eventually be necessary to control the vehicle remotely, so I installed an automatic gearbox and converted the vehicle into an automatic-manual hybrid. I chose not to make it fully automatic so that I would always have the manual option for maximum control over the vehicle whenever necessary.

October 12, 1984

Marty has asked me to help build him a mega-powered amplifier and speaker. How can I say no?

July 27, 1985

The engine rebuild and vehicle additions are successful! I drove the vehicle around Twin Pines Mall in the early hours of this morning and managed to accelerate it to 97 mph, according to my newly calibrated digital speedometer. More than enough speed for temporal displacement to be achieved.

Achmed.
555-9243

September 3, 1985

The nuclear reactor is finished. I need only one more ingredient...

September 7, 1985

I have never been one to believe in destiny, although Carl Jung's theory of synchronicity along with David Bohm's ramblings on the subject make a persuasive explanation for the message I found on my answering machine today.

September 8, 1985

Great Scott! My suspicions have been confirmed, and no amount of Pepto-Bismol has been able to settle my stomach. I told Achmed I would get back to him within 48 hours. It is the most intense quandary of my life. Consorting with Libyan nationals is problematic on every level, to say the least. Yet, if I inform the FBI, I would become the subject of an investigation myself, which would undoubtedly put a permanent end to my work and dreams. That is not an option. Could Achmed be a double-agent of some sort? No, not likely. There must be a path through this. I shall put my mind to it...

September 9, 1985

A possible course of action now occurs to me. It just might work. No—it _must_ work, as this may be my only opportunity to procure what I need.

September 12, 1985

I made it clear to Achmed that, assuming he can deliver the goods, my participation will not include ██ ██ ████████████████████

September 16, 1985

Fortunately, Edmund Scientific Supply will ship to a post office box. I can expect the radiation suits in two weeks.

October 8, 1985

This hustle is, without a doubt, the most dangerous thing I have ever done. But it's all in the name of science, and national security. Better that the key element be in my hands than in the hands of the Libyan government, or in possession of a genuine rogue scientist who could actually make good on the project...

MISSING PLUTONIUM MYSTERY SOLVED

Officials at the Pacific Nuclear Research Facility have denied a rumor that a case of plutonium is missing from their premises. A Libyan terrorist group had taken credit for allegedly stealing the highly radioactive material, but officials have now confirmed that the discrepancy was due to a clerical error.

Klaus Garcia, the facility's director, has promised a full investigation, but critics of the facility are demanding his resignation. "When it comes to nuclear material, carelessness is as bad as theft," stated Rachel Samuels of the Abolish Nuclear Power Consortium. "Have we forgotten Three Mile Island?"

October 25, 1985

Preparations are almost complete. I have now contacted Marty and enlisted his aid in my greatest experiment. I can't wait to tell him what I've been working on, and I'm hopeful that October 26, 1985, will be forever remembered as a red-letter day in the history of science! Now, where did I put my video camcorder?

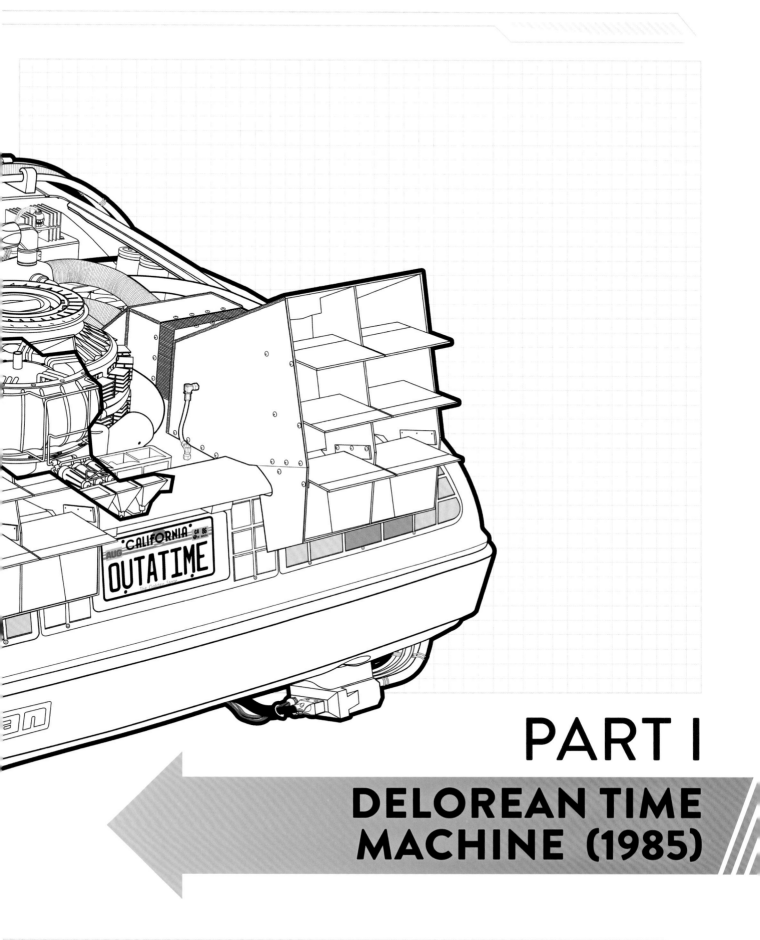

PART I

DELOREAN TIME MACHINE (1985)

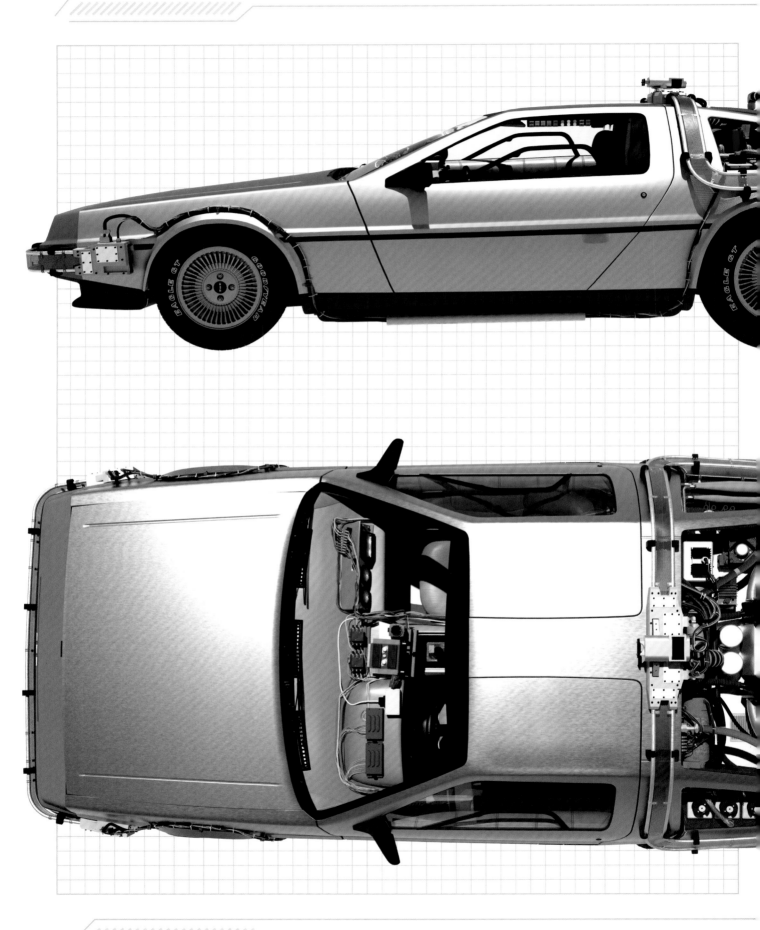

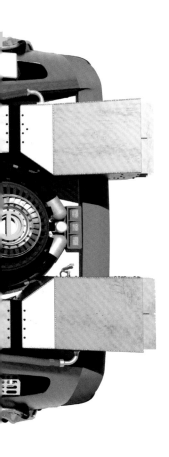

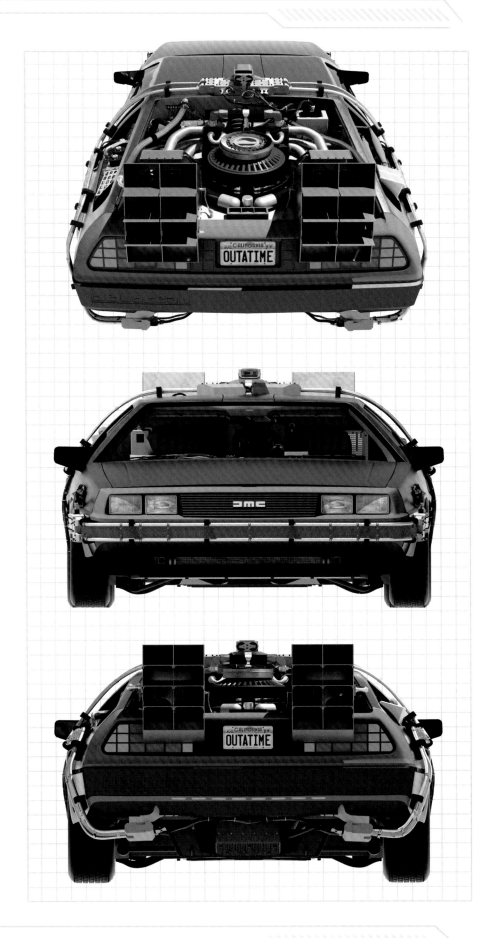

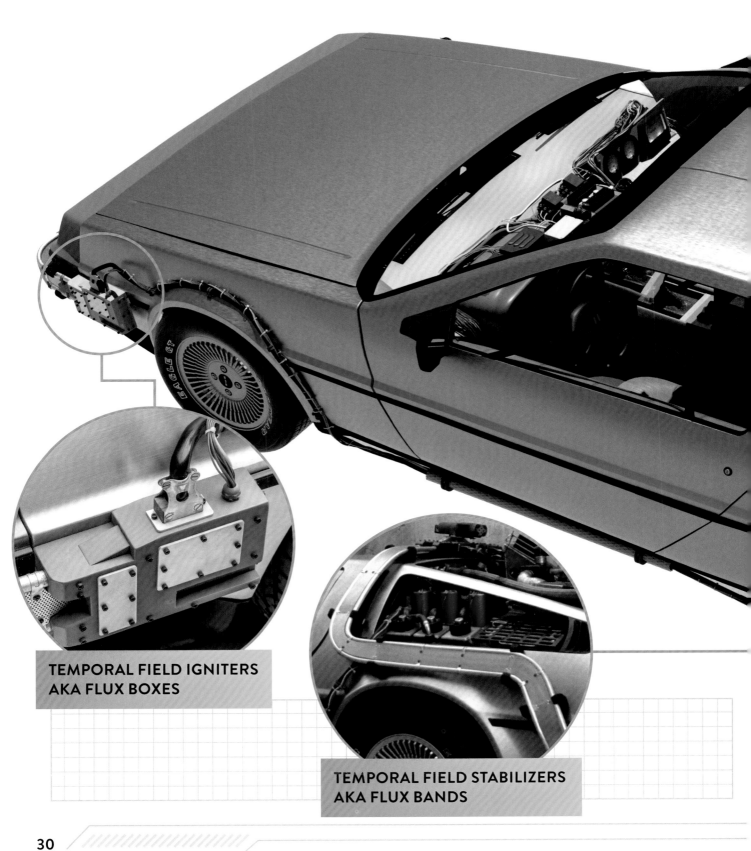

TEMPORAL FIELD IGNITERS
AKA FLUX BOXES

TEMPORAL FIELD STABILIZERS
AKA FLUX BANDS

TACHYON PULSE GENERATOR

NUCLEAR REACTOR

REACTOR COOLING VENTS

31

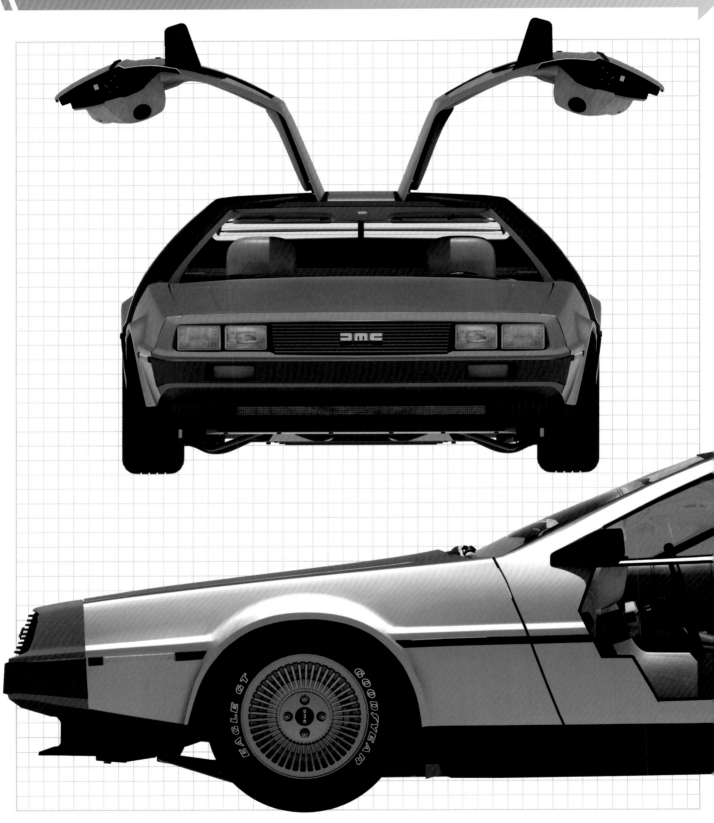

THE DELOREAN DMC-12 was designed by famed Italian automobile designer Giorgetto Giugiaro and is known for its iconic gull-wing doors and SS304 brushed stainless-steel panels. Unfortunately, its performance did not match its looks, and its stock Peugeot-Renault-Volvo 130 horsepower V6 engine was considered to be underpowered. In 1982, John DeLorean, desperate to keep his car company afloat, found himself the target of an FBI entrapment operation, which generated lots of negative attention from the media who were eager to judge him guilty. Sales of the vehicle declined over the following year, and the DeLorean Motor Company in Belfast, Northern Ireland, was forced to close its doors forever.

By the time John DeLorean was acquitted, it was too late to save the company or the car. The troubled vehicle was only available for three years, but its inspired angular stainless-steel design helped make it timeless.

The moment I laid eyes on the DeLorean DMC-12, everything clicked. After failed attempts to incorporate the time travel components into a refrigerator, a pickup truck, and a Ford Mustang, I knew instantly that this stainless beauty was the perfect host to become the time vehicle. After all, if you're going to build a time machine out of a car, why not do it with some style?

While a normal painted steel car would likely survive a temporal event, the magnetism of normal steel would negatively affect the flux dispersal. However, the stainless-steel construction of the DeLorean would serve to make the flux dispersal uniform across the entire surface area of the vehicle.

FLUX CAPACITOR

THE FLUX CAPACITOR is, in part, a ternary particle collider, but engineered with a 4th dimensional component based on ▉▉▉▉▉▉▉▉▉▉ ▉▉▉▉▉▉▉▉▉▉▉▉▉▉▉▉▉▉▉▉▉▉▉▉ ▉▉▉▉▉▉▉▉▉▉▉▉▉▉▉▉▉▉▉▉▉▉▉▉ ▉▉▉▉▉▉▉▉▉▉▉▉▉▉▉▉▉▉▉▉▉▉▉ ▉▉▉▉▉▉▉▉▉▉▉▉▉▉▉▉▉▉▉ ▉▉▉▉▉▉▉▉▉▉▉▉▉▉▉▉▉▉ Thus, given an application of directed electrical energy, it enables the creation of one of the most elusive particles in physics which, in 1962, was dubbed a "tachyon."

The generated tachyons are contained within the flux capacitor until a high enough concentration is achieved.

At this point, when coupled with conditions including ▉▉▉▉▉▉▉▉▉▉▉▉▉▉▉▉▉▉▉▉ ▉▉▉▉▉▉▉▉▉▉▉▉▉▉▉▉, tachyon particles are released, which, when properly focused, can create a wormhole and open a portal through the time continuum.

The energy release is potentially blinding. Caution is required at all times.

FLUX CAPACITOR COMPONENTS

1. 11" x 13" x 5" ELECTRONICS ENCLOSURE
2. PARTICLE COLLIDER BLADES
3. COLLISION SYNCHRONIZERS
4. GEIGER-MÜLLER TUBE (RADIATION DETECTOR)
5. TACHYON PULSE GENERATOR CONTROL (CANON 32)
6. EXHAUST ELBOW (TO EXTERNAL EXHAUST DUCT)
7. TIME CIRCUITS CONTROL (CANON 20)
8. FLUX CAPACITOR COOLANT

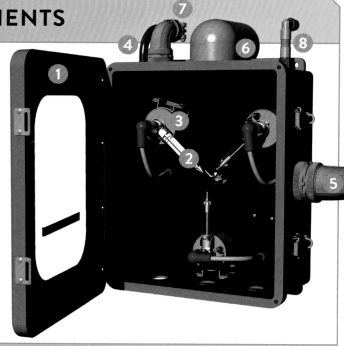

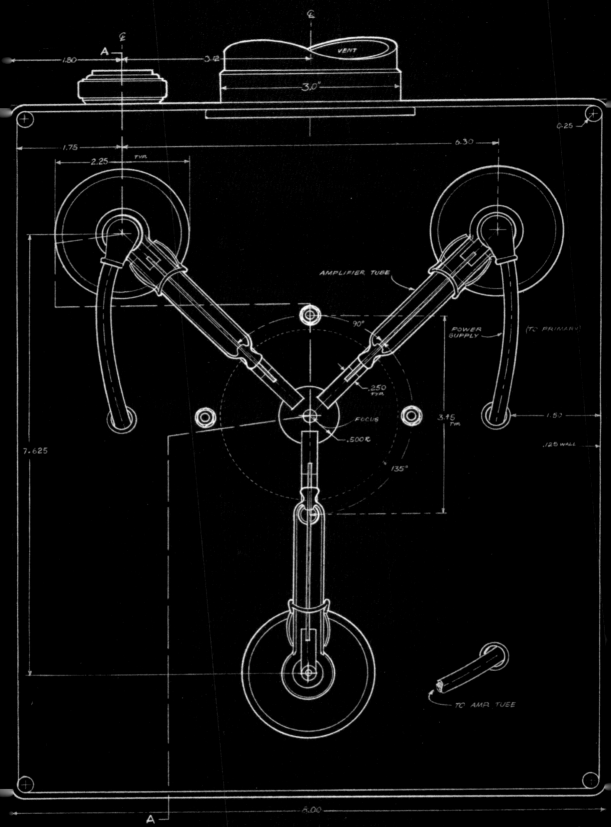

VENT

3.0"

A

1.80

3.12

1.75

6.30

0.25

2.25

TYP.

AMPLIFIER TUBE

90°

POWER
SUPPLY

(TO PRIMARY)

.250
TYP.

FOCUS

3.45
TYP.

1.50

.125 WALL

.500 R

135°

7.625

TO AMP. TUBE

A

6.00

FRONT VIEW

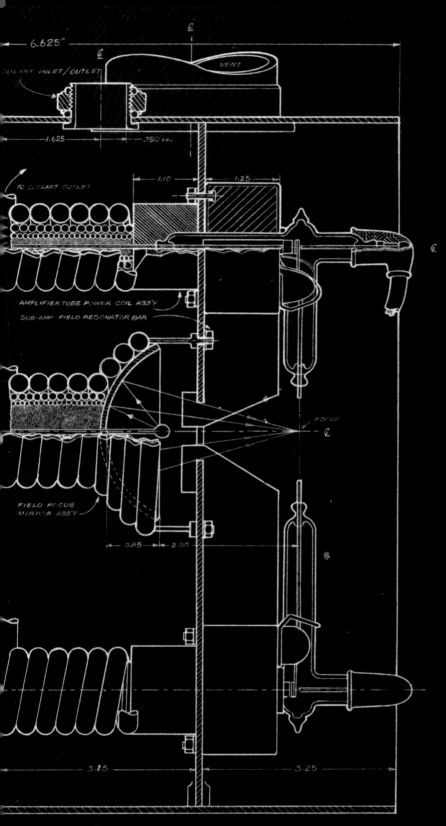

6.625"

COOLANT INLET/OUTLET

VENT

1.625

.750 I.D.

TO COOLANT OUTLET

1.10

1.25

AMPLIFIER TUBE POWER COIL ASS'Y

SUB-AMP FIELD RESONATOR BAR

FOCUS

FIELD FOCUS
MIRROR ASS'Y

0.85

2.00

3.15

3.25

SECTION A·A

TEMPORAL FIELD
CAPACITOR

PRELIMINARY ASS'Y
SCHEMATIC

FULL SCALE	DRAWN BY:
CONFIDENTIAL	DATE:

TACHYON PULSE GENERATOR

THE TACHYON PULSE GENERATOR (TPG) fires tachyons at and through the electromagnetic field, targeted at the exact relative distance ahead of the field in which the vehicle will travel at the optimal speed.

By firing tachyons through the temporal field, the field becomes primed for contact with the wormhole. If 1.21 gigawatts of electricity is introduced at the exact moment the temporal field touches the wormhole, the time vehicle passes through instantly and disappears with an implosion that leaves behind a vacuum that the surrounding air rushes to fill.

Eighty-eight miles per hour is the ideal temporal displacement threshold, although successful temporal displacement can occur at greater speeds. A minimum safe distance is required between the time vehicle and the wormhole as it is being generated. The wormhole is only open momentarily, therefore, the vehicle must be traveling at the correct speed in order to cover the distance required for the temporal field and wormhole to converge.

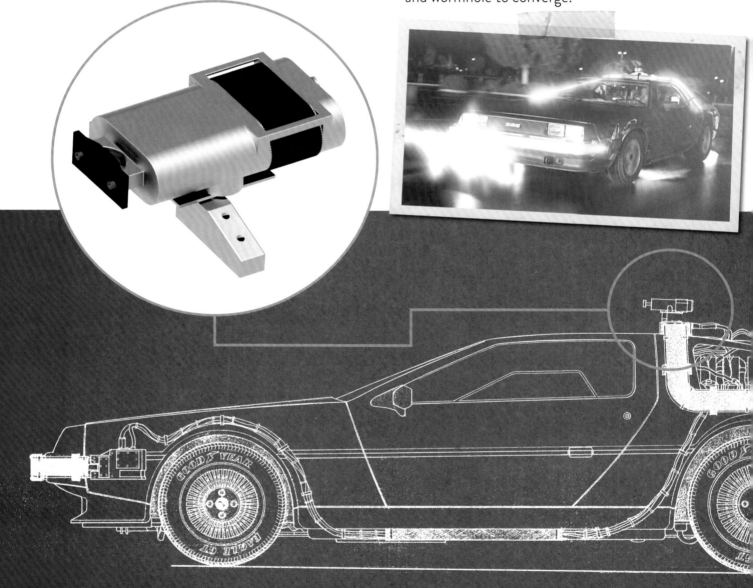

"WHAT THE HELL IS A GIGAWATT?"

A kilowatt is one thousand watts.
A megawatt is one million watts.
A gigawatt is one billion watts.

HOW IS IT PRONOUNCED: GIGA-WATT OR JIGA-WATT?

Although the prefix "giga" is usually pronounced with a hard "g," it's derived from the Greek "gigos" (pronounced "jie-goes"), the root of "gigantic." So both the soft "g" and hard "g" pronunciations are correct.

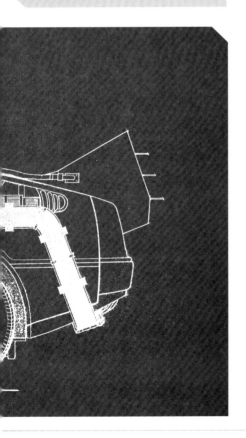

TEMPORAL DISPLACEMENT SYSTEM

The space-time continuum maintains a constant state of perfect equilibrium. Temporal events emit so much negative energy that at the moment the time vehicle enters the wormhole, it is extremely hot.

The transfer of momentum between molecular particles causes the time vehicle to return with an equal amount of positive energy, which displaces the surrounding energy.

The end result is an instantaneous sub-freezing atmosphere surrounding the vehicle upon re-entry. I had not calculated that the time travel temperature differential would result in an ice-covered vehicle. In subsequent temporal traveling, the ice was minimal, and sometimes non-existent, leading me to conclude that it is a function of the humidity and water vapor in the air at the destination.

1. NUCLEAR REACTOR
2. REACTOR POWER COILS
3. PARTICLE ACCELERATION CANISTERS
4. FLUX CAPACITOR (INSIDE)
5. TACHYON PULSE GENERATOR

PARTICLE ACCELERATOR CANISTERS (PAC)

THERE ARE THREE Particle Accelerator Canisters, one for each of the three collider blades in the flux capacitor. These canisters accelerate the particles to astronomical speeds prior to being introduced into the flux capacitor.

These PACs are not as powerful as their lengthier Hadron counterparts in Switzerland, but they are more efficient, require less power to operate, and are, most importantly, portable.

The accelerators produce beams of supercharged particles that are then directed through insulated conduits, which feed into the flux capacitor. The three accelerators must remain absolutely uniform and balanced while each utilizing independent power coils. Therefore, a dedicated power regulation system controls the trio in unison.

PAC COMPONENTS

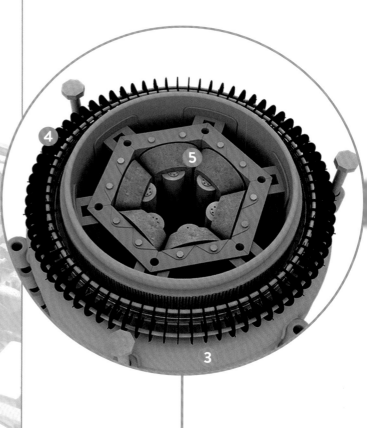

TO FLUX CAPACITOR

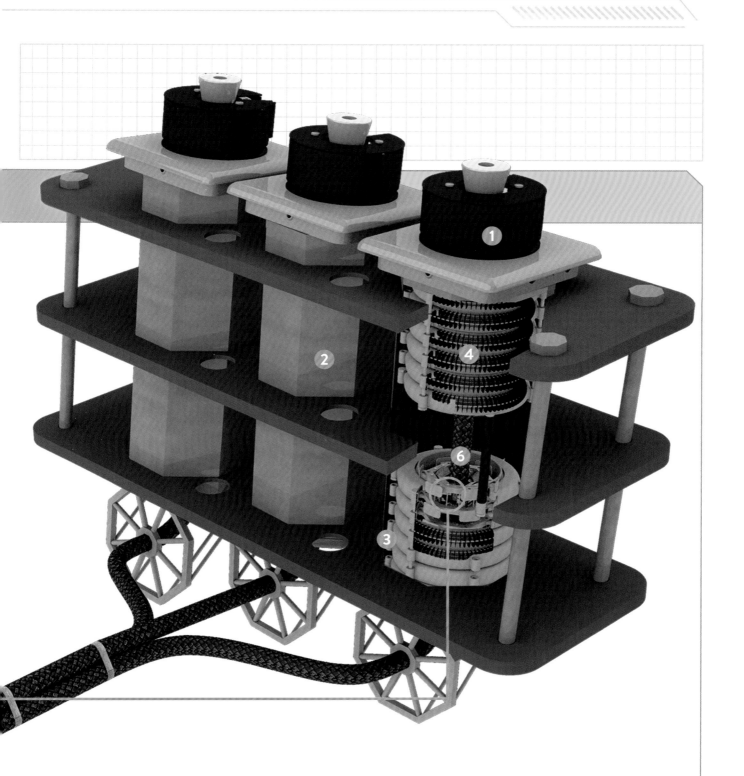

1. PAC (PARTICLE
   ACCELERATOR CANISTERS)
2. SHIELDED ENCLOSURE
3. PROTECTIVE CASING
4. ELECTROMAGNET RINGS
5. BENDING/FOCUSING MAGNETS
6. PARTICLE BEAM CONDUIT

TIME CIRCUITS DISPLAY

Before I could create the Time Circuits Computer, I had to solve one more significant problem. Consider: if you depart in a time machine from, say, town square in Hill Valley, and travel ten minutes into the future, will you arrive in town square or, due to the rotation of the earth, find yourself several miles out of town? For that matter, would you find yourself several miles in outer space or a few miles underground? The Earth not only rotates, but it revolves around the Sun. In fact, everything in the Universe is in constant motion and expansion, and, as Einstein told us, there is no known point of reference to pinpoint how anything is moving in relation to everything else. A very powerful computer would have to calculate each journey based on every known relative quantity and, without precise calculations, the trip might end more abruptly than anticipated.

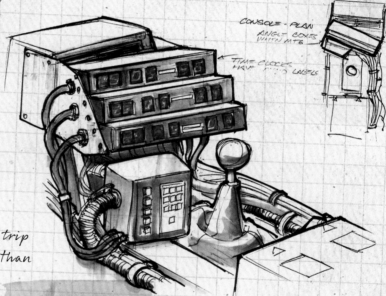

CONSOLE - PLAN
ANGLE BOXES
WITH MTG

TIME CLOCKS
HAVE FIXED LABELS

bass — volume — off

st

am fm

54 70 90 120 160
88 92 96 100 104 108

auto - stop

stereo cassette reciever

am fm fm/st

treble — tune

Airguide

S SE
150 120

MONTH **NOV** DAY **05** YEAR **1955** AM PM HOUR **06** MIN **00**

DESTINATION TIME

MONTH **OCT** DAY **26** YEAR **1985** AM PM HOUR **06** MIN **23**

PRESENT TIME

MONTH **OCT** DAY **26** YEAR **1985** AM PM HOUR **01** MIN **35**

LAST TIME DEPARTED

1 2 3
4 5 6
7 8 9
0

See next page!

DISPLAY COMPONENTS

1. TIME CIRCUITS DISPLAY ENCLOSURE
2. DESTINATION TIME DISPLAY
3. TRW DATA SYSTEMS KEYPAD
4. COUSTIC EI AM/FM CASSETTE RADIO
5. AIRGUIDE AUTO COMPASS
6. POWER REGULATOR PCB & HEAT SINK

However, that's just one theory. There's also Brown's Theory of Temporal Relativity, which states, "If you travel in time, you are universally tethered to the exact point from which you left, no matter 'when' you go or how far the Earth has rotated or traveled through space." This, we assume, is because nature abhors a vacuum and the Universe does not lose track of anything. After all, a change in your physical location would be considered teleportation, and, according to known laws of physics, that's simply not possible. In H.G. Wells' <u>The Time Machine</u>, it was Temporal Relativity that allowed his Time Traveler to sit and watch the years pass, watching the progress of mankind in fast-forward.

The best analogy is to a housefly on a moving bus. The fly sits on top of a seat, yet when it flies, it does not get smashed by the rear window of the bus speeding forward behind it. Instead, its position remains relative to that of the bus. From the fly's perspective, the movement of the bus is irrelevant. And from the time traveler's perspective, celestial motion is irrelevant.

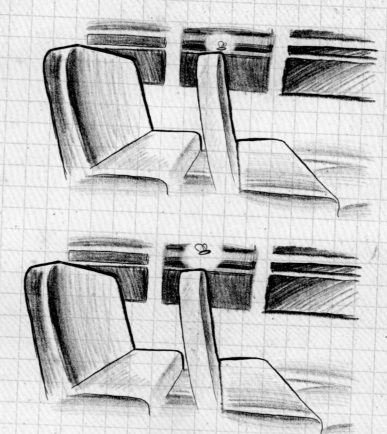

That theory meant that the primary purpose of the time circuit computer would be to adjust and compensate for discrepancies between the Gregorian and Julian calendars and, in more recent times, daylight savings time.

GREGORIAN/JULIAN CALENDAR CORRECTION

The Gregorian calendar was initiated in 1582, replacing the Julian calendar, which had incorrectly calculated the length of a year at 365.25 days instead of 365.2425 days. The difference required a correction of 10 days, so that October 4, 1582 was followed by October 15, 1582. The time vehicle's computer is calibrated to use the Gregorian calendar for all dates following October 4, 1582, and the Julian calendar for dates prior.

I used a simple telephone-style keypad as the input device to set the destination time. When a month-day-year combination (with time of day optional) is numerically entered, the destination time display lights up with the information. I opted for the standard American style array with three-letter month abbreviations in the first position, followed by the day and the year, along with the 12-hour time and a.m./p.m. indicator, simply because I always thought of dates and times in this format. I limited the annum display to four digits, allowing me to travel across 10,000 years. Thus, a trip to the Mesozoic era to observe dinosaurs will require an upgrade.

As an homage to one of my favorite movies, I color-coded the displays red (destination time), green (present time), and yellow (last time departed), because these were the colors of the bulbs on director George Pal's "Time Machine" control system.

TIME CIRCUITS SWITCH CONSOLE

THIS CONSOLE USES a simple, low-tech housing, built from tempered reinforced steel for protection of the all-important Time Circuits.

1. **TIME CIRCUITS COMPUTER**
2. **"Y" HANDLE SWITCH**
3. **DIALCO INDICATOR LIGHTS**
4. **EMERGENCY SYSTEM RESET**
5. **PRIMARY FREQUENCY CONTROL**
6. **RELOCATED DMC SWITCHES**
7. **CLARE ELECTROSEAL CONSTANT POWER SUPPLY**
8. **MOTOR RUN CAPACITORS**
9. **HIGH-VOLTAGE TRANSFORMER**
10. **SPRAGUE CAPACITORS**
11. **MANUAL COMPONENTS CONTROL**
12. **MANUAL EMERGENCY COOLANT RELEASE**

FLUX BANDS
AKA TEMPORAL FIELD STABILIZERS

THE FLUX BANDS contain and define the temporal field, so proper calibration and placement around the vehicle is vital. In addition, the bands are reinforced to act as a debris shield for the more fragile temporal field helix.

Three flux bands surround the car. One band wraps around the front bumper, defining the front of the field and preventing it from extending too far forward or back.

The two remaining bands start from the top of the DeLorean, make a 90-degree turn toward the rear of the vehicle and wrap underneath the stern.

The blue glow of the flux bands is plasma discharge resulting from friction between the temporal field and the fully charged flux bands.

The other point of contact between the vehicle and the temporal field are the tires.

They must travel through time with the vehicle while the pavement must be left behind, meaning the margin of error is just a few microns.

Because the tires are in contact with the perimeter of the temporal field, they leave behind a thin layer of hyper-excited field particles, which ignite upon contact with the air and appear as flame trails.

Flame trails occur whether the car is traveling on the ground or in the air. The tires on the hover-converted DeLorean fold 90 degrees, where they come in contact with the side of the temporal field (see part 2 for details.).

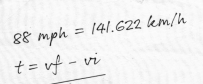

$88 \text{ mph} = 141.622 \text{ km/h}$

Test Acceleration
$0 - 88$ in ?

$t = \dfrac{vf - vi}{a}$

$w = A \times V$ $\quad \sqrt{P \times R}$

$P = 1.21 \text{ gw}$

$P = \dfrac{E}{T}$

Using the DeLorean's unique shape to envelop the time vehicle in a perfectly formed temporal field was a geometric problem that could have stumped Pythagoras.

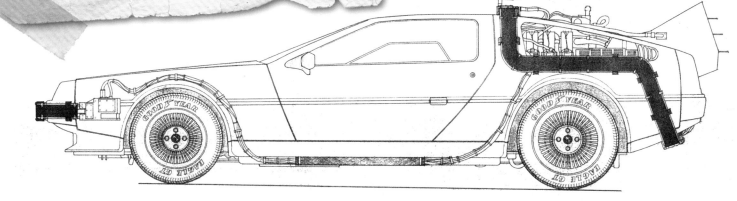

FIELD CONTAINMENT SYSTEM

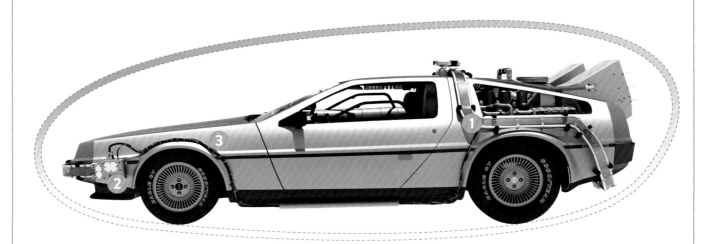

THE FIELD CONTAINMENT SYSTEM, which is powered by the internal combustion engine, creates and contains an electromagnetic bubble, a primer field that becomes a temporal field when tachyon particles are introduced. The temporal field surrounds the entire vehicle, allowing everything inside the field to travel safely through time. Without containment, the temporal field is nebulous and can be unpredictable. If you tried to travel through time without a complete Field Containment System, it's conceivable that only half of the vehicle, or half of your body, might be transported. A one-way trip, indeed.

1 **TEMPORAL FIELD STABILIZERS**

2 **TEMPORAL FIELD IGNITION BOXES**

3 **MOLE RICHARDSON POWER CABLES**

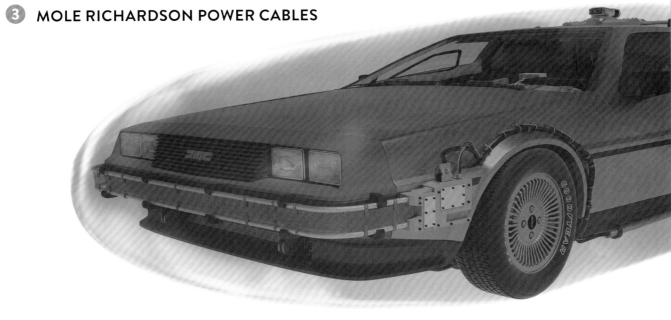

FLUX BOXES
(TEMPORAL FIELD IGNITION BOXES)

THERE ARE SIX flux boxes on the time vehicle: two mounted to the front quarter panels, two mounted on the roof, and two beneath the vehicle in the rear. These boxes are custom electronics enclosures that house temporal field ignition coils.

The field ignition coils are fed excited tachyons that transform the electromagnetic field into a temporal field. Time travel cannot be achieved safely without a stable temporal field.

FLUX BOX COMPONENTS

1. FIELD IGNITION COILS
2. CONTROL CIRCUITS
3. PULSE GENERATORS
4. X-RAY TUBES
5. SURGE PROTECTOR
6. POWER INPUT (MOLE RICHARDSON 100 AMP FEMALE)
7. HIGH VOLTAGE CABLE CLAMPS
8. BOOSTER COIL
9. SHIELDED SPARK GAP CHAMBER
10. LOAD RESISTOR
11. ARGON-GAS-FILLED TUBES
12. CATHODE WITH SPARK GENERATOR
13. ANODE
14. SPARK GAP INSIDE PROTECTIVE GLASS SHEILD

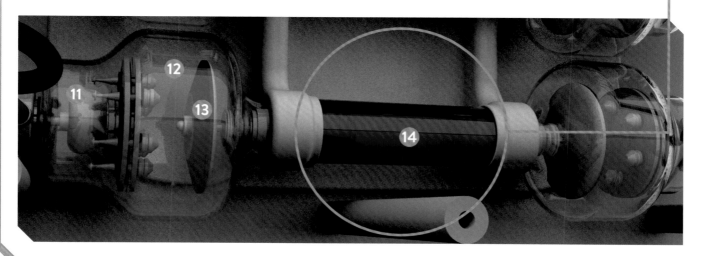

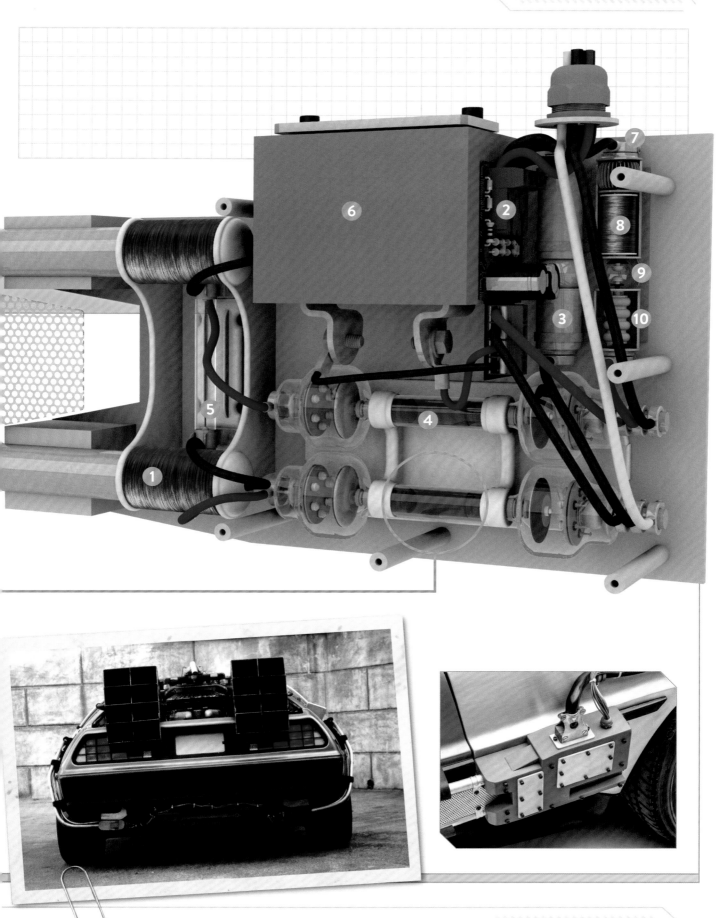

NUCLEAR REACTOR

Inside the trapezoidal enclosure on the front of the reactor is the unit's steam-powered generator. Steam created by the heat from the reactor passes through the generator's turbines and creates electricity. The steam then passes from one cooling system to the next, ultimately through the condensers inside the vents. The liquid is collected and reintroduced into the primary coolant pump.

The DeLorean Time Machine requires a nuclear reactor to deliver 1.21 gigawatts of electricity to hyper-excite the temporal field, resulting in the opening of a wormhole. Therefore, I created the world's first rapid decay reactor, in an ultra compact size.

Of course, a nuclear reactor of this kind is incredibly dangerous and requires constant monitoring and a substantial network of cooling systems and vents, including a liquid Freon emergency cooling system to counteract the unlikely event of a reactor meltdown. My added precaution is a non-conducting water-based super coolant "cocktail." Without a super coolant, a fast reaction is impossible to cool at normal atmospheric pressure.

Everything in the vicinity of the plutonium chamber is lead lined. You can never be too safe.

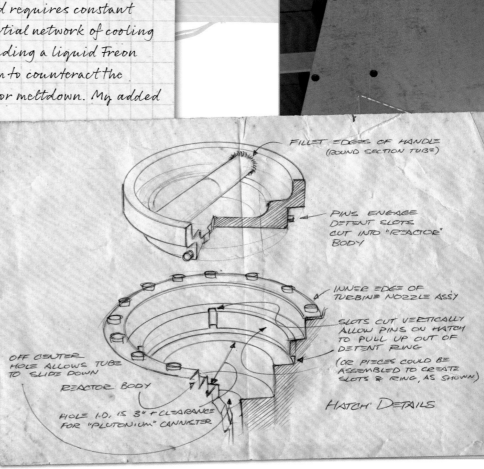

FILLET EDGES OF HANDLE
(ROUND SECTION TUBE)

PINS ENGAGE DETENT SLOTS CUT INTO "REACTOR" BODY

INNER EDGE OF TURBINE NOZZLE ASSY

SLOTS CUT VERTICALLY ALLOW PINS ON HATCH TO PULL UP OUT OF DETENT RING

(OR PIECES COULD BE ASSEMBLED TO CREATE SLOTS & RING, AS SHOWN)

HATCH DETAILS

OFF CENTER HOLE ALLOWS TUBE TO SLIDE DOWN

REACTOR BODY

HOLE I.D. IS 3" + CLEARANCE FOR "PLUTONIUM" CANNISTER

NUCLEAR REACTOR COMPONENTS

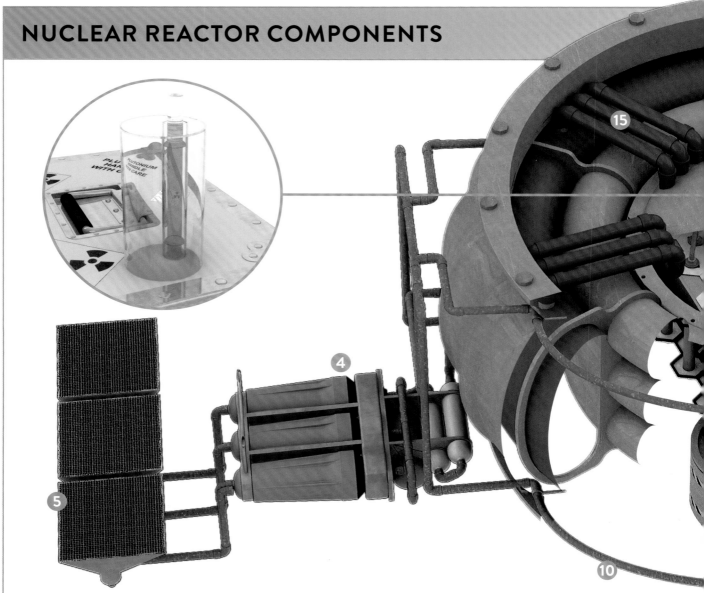

1. REACTOR CORE
2. REACTOR OUTER HOUSING
3. FREON INJECTION NOZZLES AND EXPANSION CHAMBER
4. RADIATION SCRUBBER
5. RADIATION SCRUBBER VENT
6. REMOVABLE SPENT-PLUTONIUM CANISTER (LEAD LINED)
7. GENERATORS
8. ████████ COOLANT INLETS
9. STEAM TURBINES
10. STEAM EXHAUST AND RECYCLING TUBES (TO RADIATION SCRUBBER)
11. COOLANT PURGE TUBES
12. STEAM FEED TUBE FOR TURBINES
13. MEDIUM PRESSURE BOILERS
14. HIGH PRESSURE BOILERS
15. REACTOR CORE COOLING
16. COOLING RING

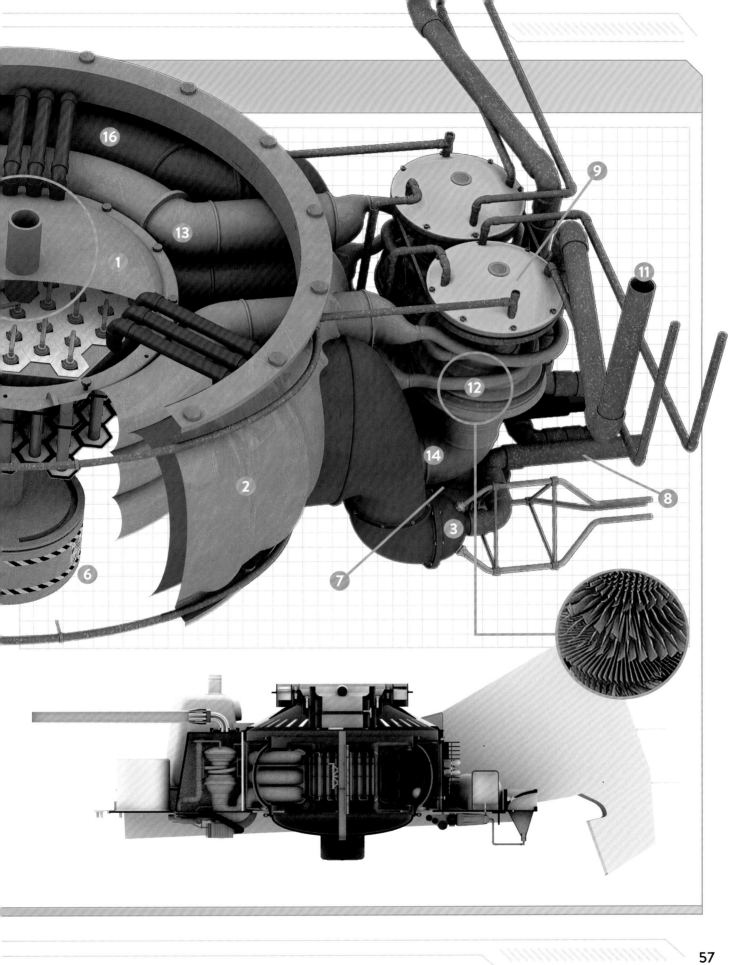

REACTOR COILS

REACTOR COIL EXTERIOR

THE REACTOR COILS are located directly in front of the nuclear reactor steam-powered generator. These coils store all of the electricity generated by the reactor prior to the temporal event.

1. **REACTOR COIL ENCLOSURES**
2. **REACTOR COILS**
3. **CERAMIC SEPARATOR & CONDUCTIVE SPRING**
4. **LOWER REACTOR COILS ASSEMBLY**
5. **COIL ASSEMBLY PLATE (MOUNTS TO UNDERSIDE OF ENGINE COVER)**

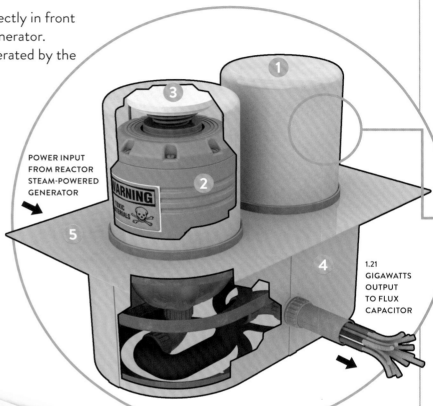

POWER INPUT FROM REACTOR STEAM-POWERED GENERATOR

WARNING TOXIC MATERIALS

1.21 GIGAWATTS OUTPUT TO FLUX CAPACITOR

REACTOR COIL INTERIOR

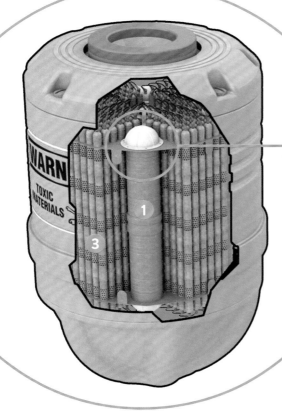

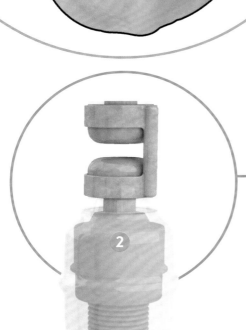

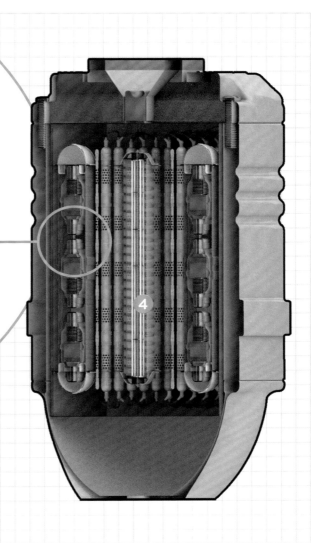

1. VACUUM CAPACITORS CHAMBER
2. 5MW VACUUM CAPACITORS
3. BATTERY CELL CORES
4. PRIMARY COIL IN VACUUM CHAMBER

REACTOR COOLING VENTS

THE REACTOR COOLING VENTS serve the same function as the cooling towers at nuclear power plants, helping to regulate the temperature, keeping the reactor cool, and purging excess heat. These custom vents also contain heat exchangers and condensers to maximize efficiency.

The moving parts inside the vents are controlled by hydraulics, as is the plutonium pellet-handling system inside the reactor itself.

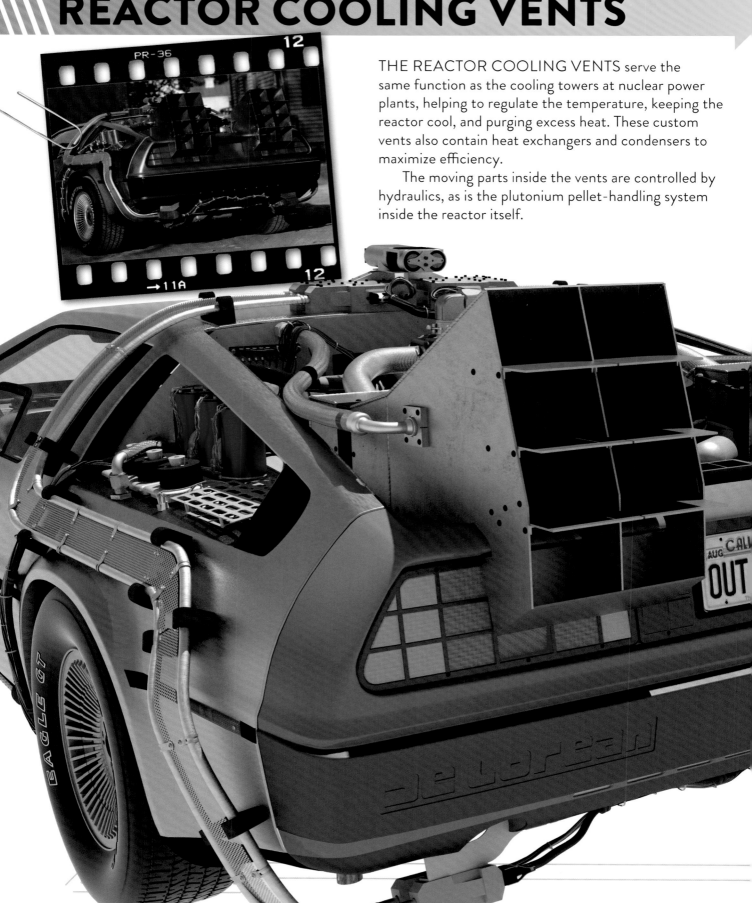

EMERGENCY COOLING SYSTEM

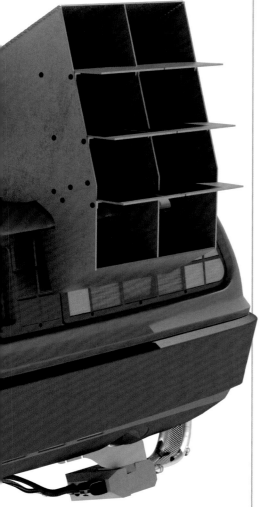

THE THREE GREEN accumulator tubes mounted in the passenger side pontoon are filled with liquid Freon. The Freon is fed through high-pressure stainless steel tubes into the Thermal Control Unit, which distributes and regulates all the coolant. The emergency cryogenic solenoids are triggered in the event of an impending emergency, and liquid Freon is directly injected into the reactor, causing instant condensation. This creates excess pressure that the system must purge through the vents, blanketing the ground with a cold layer of gas.

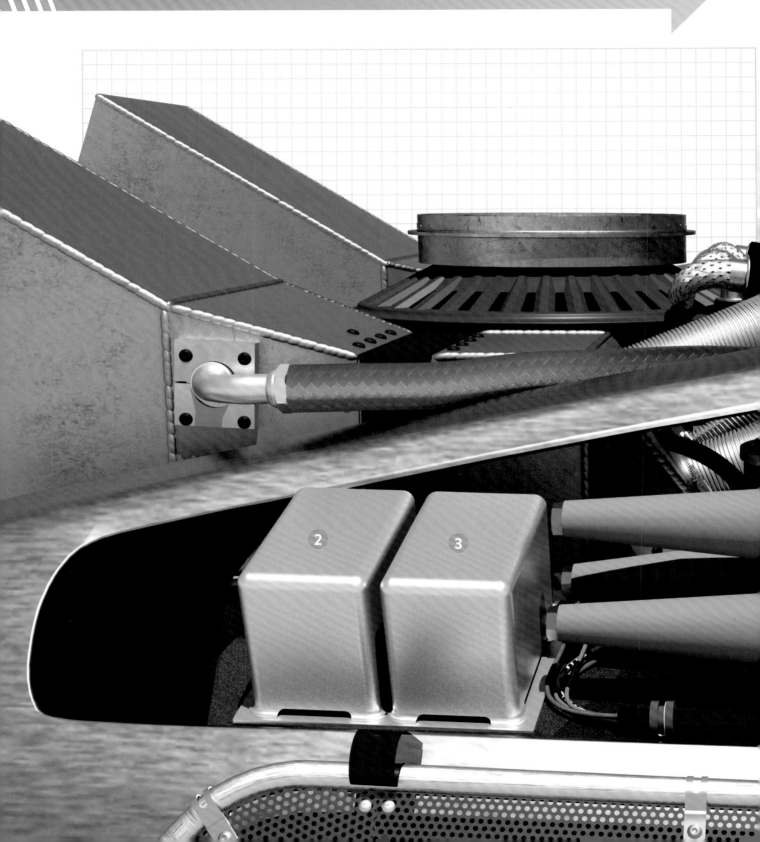

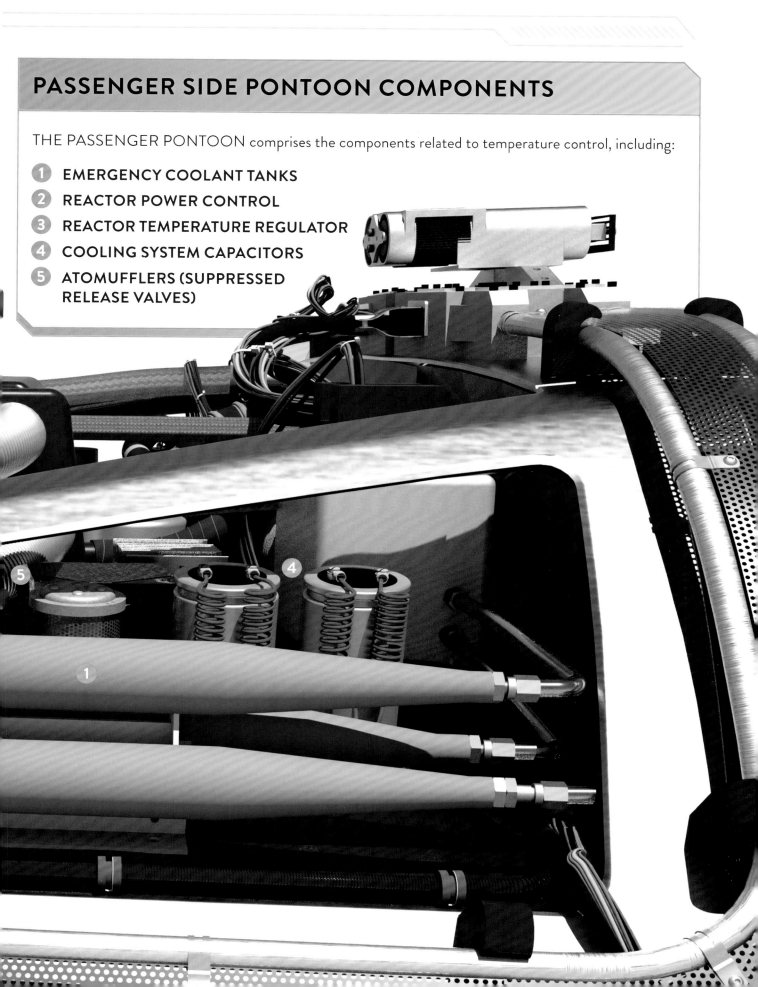

PASSENGER SIDE PONTOON COMPONENTS

THE PASSENGER PONTOON comprises the components related to temperature control, including:

1. **EMERGENCY COOLANT TANKS**
2. **REACTOR POWER CONTROL**
3. **REACTOR TEMPERATURE REGULATOR**
4. **COOLING SYSTEM CAPACITORS**
5. **ATOMUFFLERS (SUPPRESSED RELEASE VALVES)**

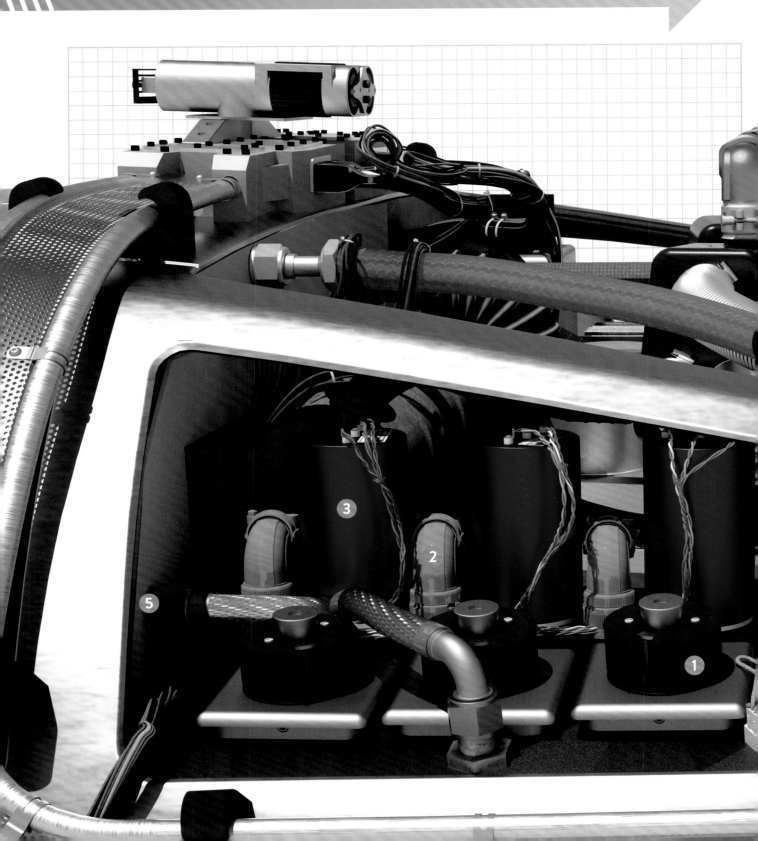

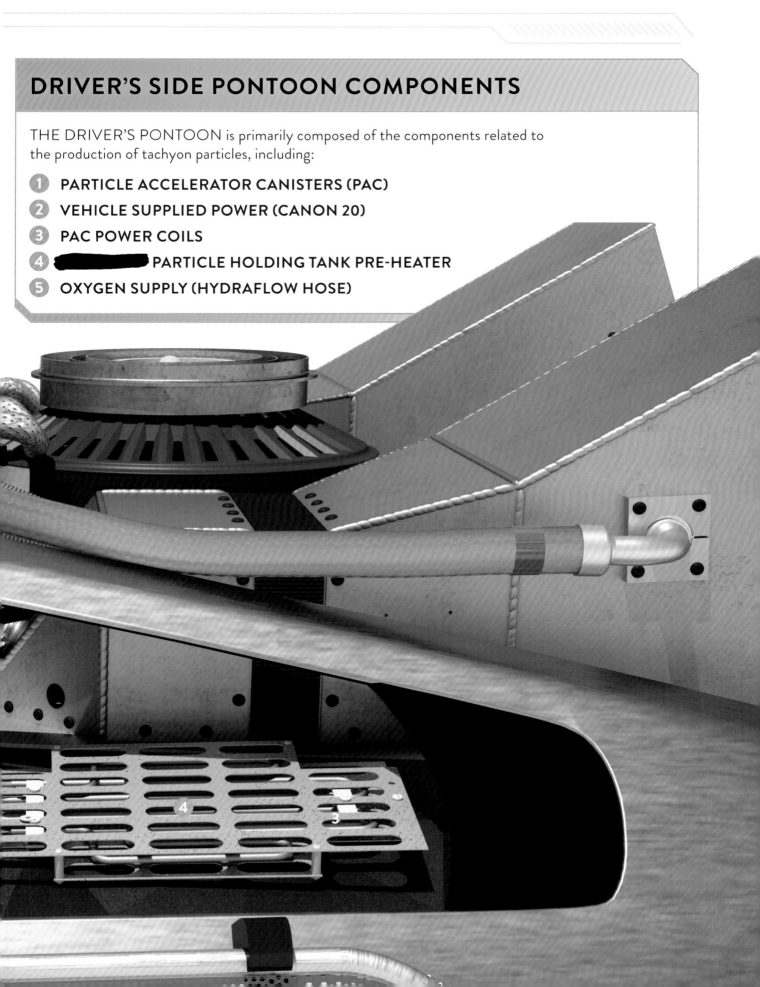

DRIVER'S SIDE PONTOON COMPONENTS

THE DRIVER'S PONTOON is primarily composed of the components related to the production of tachyon particles, including:

1. **PARTICLE ACCELERATOR CANISTERS (PAC)**
2. **VEHICLE SUPPLIED POWER (CANON 20)**
3. **PAC POWER COILS**
4. ██████████ **PARTICLE HOLDING TANK PRE-HEATER**
5. **OXYGEN SUPPLY (HYDRAFLOW HOSE)**

BULKHEAD

THE VEHICLE'S REAR WINDOW had to be removed and replaced with a reinforced aluminum bulkhead to support the many Time Machine components, the most important of which is the flux capacitor. The Field Containment System Display, otherwise known as the "Christmas Tree," is mounted so that it is clear of the driver's seat, as will be explained on page 75.

BULKHEAD COMPONENTS

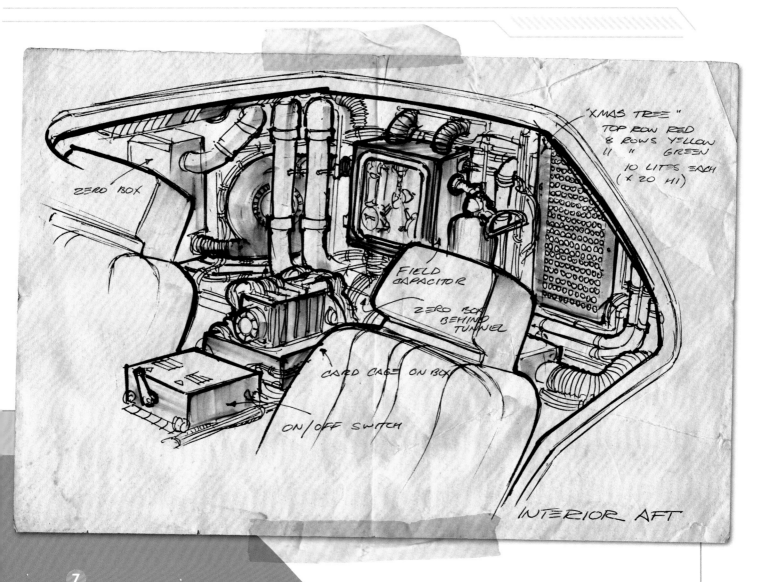

1. TIME CIRCUITS CONTROL JUNCTION
2. TIME CIRCUITS WARM-UP RELAYS
3. REACTOR THERMAL CONTROL UNIT
4. TORIN CORPORATION BLOWER
5. FLUX CAPACITOR
6. CABIN ATMOSPHERE & FIRE CONTROL
7. PULSE CONTROL MODULE
8. FIELD CONTAINMENT SYSTEM DISPLAY

REACTOR THERMAL CONTROL UNIT

THIS EQUIPMENT, MOUNTED behind the passenger seat, is directly connected to the nuclear reactor's thermal monitoring and emergency cooling systems. Positioned out of the driver's line of sight, each yellow indicator is equipped with a unique emergency warning tone that alerts the driver to significant changes in temperature or radiation levels.

1. THERMAL COMMUNICATION RELAY (CANON 20)
2. EMERGENCY COOLING SYSTEM THERMOSTAT
3. SYSTEM STATUS INDICATORS

EXTERIOR BULKHEAD LEDGE

THE WEATHER-PROTECTED COMPONENTS on the exterior bulkhead ledge, with the exception of the flux capacitor exhaust, serve the nuclear reactor's cooling system. It was essential that they be mounted externally to expose them to air and thereby actuate heat dissipation.

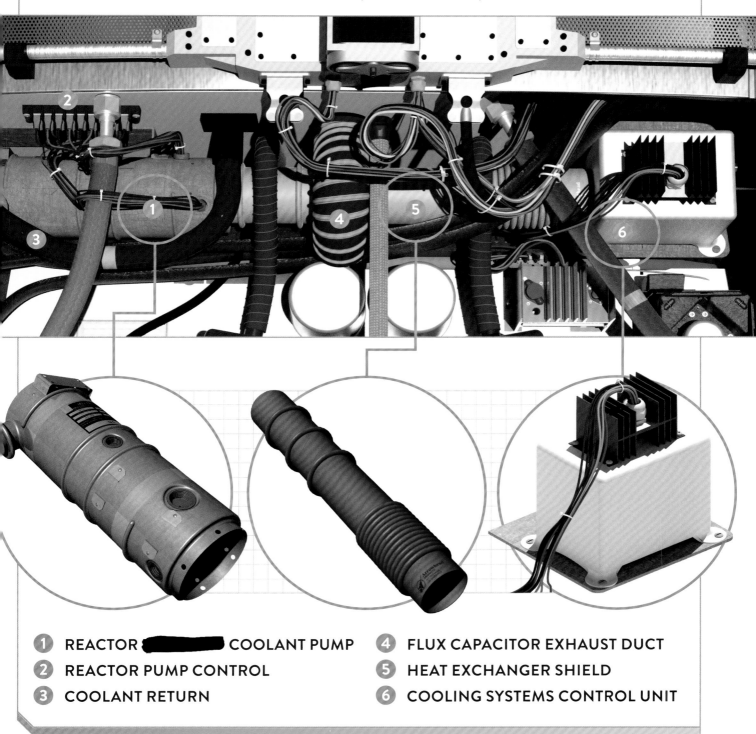

1. REACTOR ███████ COOLANT PUMP
2. REACTOR PUMP CONTROL
3. COOLANT RETURN
4. FLUX CAPACITOR EXHAUST DUCT
5. HEAT EXCHANGER SHIELD
6. COOLING SYSTEMS CONTROL UNIT

DASHBOARD

THE VEHICLE'S DASHBOARD has been augmented with Time Machine specific displays and equipment, a calibrated digital speedometer, and gauges to monitor the nuclear reactor. Of particular importance is the Roentgens meter designed to inform the time traveler of radiation levels.

DASHBOARD COMPONENTS

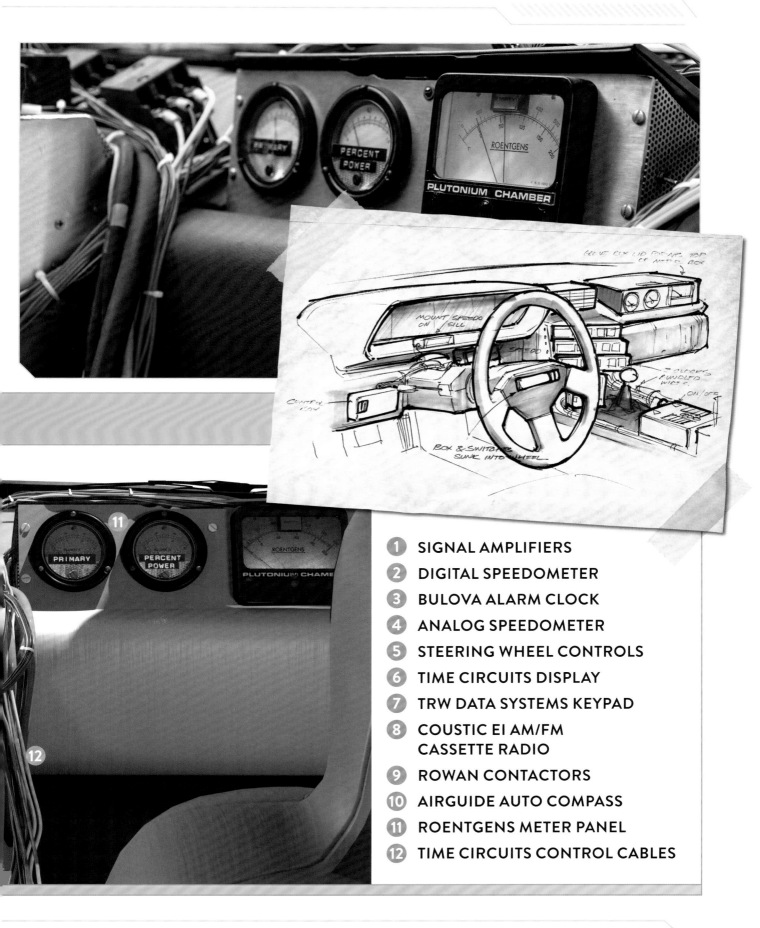

1. SIGNAL AMPLIFIERS
2. DIGITAL SPEEDOMETER
3. BULOVA ALARM CLOCK
4. ANALOG SPEEDOMETER
5. STEERING WHEEL CONTROLS
6. TIME CIRCUITS DISPLAY
7. TRW DATA SYSTEMS KEYPAD
8. COUSTIC EI AM/FM CASSETTE RADIO
9. ROWAN CONTACTORS
10. AIRGUIDE AUTO COMPASS
11. ROENTGENS METER PANEL
12. TIME CIRCUITS CONTROL CABLES

DASHBOARD ACCESSORIES

AIRGUIDE AUTO COMPASS

COUSTIC EI AM/FM CASSETTE RADIO

BULOVA ALARM CLOCK

DIGITAL SPEEDOMETER

OTHER CABIN CONTROLS

CABIN ATMOSPHERE & FIRE SUPPRESSION

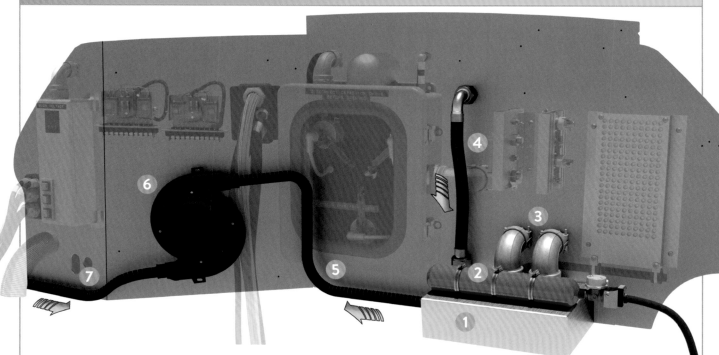

THE ATMOSPHERE CONTROL system regulates both temperature and barometric pressure, maintaining the cabin at a steady 70 degrees Fahrenheit and 101.325 kilopascals (14.696 psi). This system was included as a precaution against the possibility of time traveling to an era in which a disaster (natural or man-made) had wreaked havoc with the environment.

1. **ATMOSPHERE CONTROL REGULATOR**
2. **FIRE SUPPRESSION BOTTLE**
3. **AIR QUALITY & TEMPERATURE SENSORS (CANON 32)**
4. **OXYGEN SUPPLY**
5. **REGULATED OXYGEN TO TORIN BLOWER**
6. **TORIN BLOWER**
7. **REGULATED NITROGEN TO TORIN BLOWER**

OVERHEAD ARRAY

THE LIGHTS IN the overhead array apply mainly to the nuclear reactor systems, providing color-coded status indicators for the steam turbines and power systems. The indicators and switches allow the systems to be monitored and manually overridden in case of an emergency.

1. **SYSTEM INDICATORS (PRIMARY BANK)**
2. **SYSTEM INDICATORS (SECONDARY BANKS)**
3. **OVERHEAD ARRAY CIRCUITS**
4. **POWER DISTRIBUTION**
5. **GRIMES EMERGENCY PULL LIGHT (REMOVABLE)**

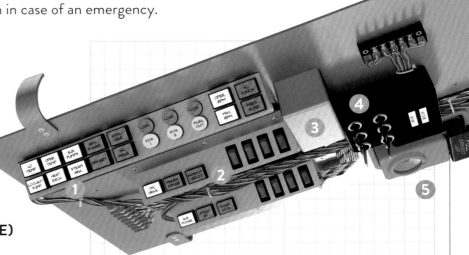

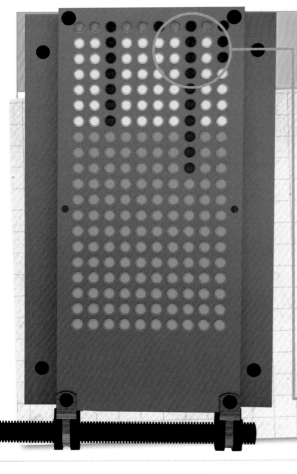

FIELD CONTAINMENT SYSTEM DISPLAY

This display graphically presents key information about the temporal field stabilizers and the temporal field ignition boxes. It may seem strange for such a display to be installed behind the driver's seat and thus out of sight, but appearances can be deceiving. With dashboard space at a premium, I was forced to create a heads-up-style display that, when mounted at the perfect angle, reflects the lighted display off the windshield directly back at the driver.

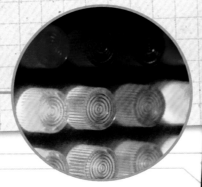

ENGINE COVER

THE STOCK DELOREAN engine cover was replaced by a custom, reinforced para-magnetic lead-lined aluminum structure that supports and accommodates the nuclear reactor and its systems while not adding any unnecessary weight. This contributes virtually no magnetic interference to the temporal fields, making it possible to accurately form, balance, and disperse the field during a temporal event.

Aluminum does possess a slight magnetic attraction, as does stainless steel, although it's not typically observable due to the strong gravitational force of the Earth. In fact, the relative permeability of aluminum is just 1.000021 whereas the relative permeability of typical vehicle steel (not stainless) is on the order of 1,000 or greater.

Vehicle tests of conventional steel vehicles provided dangerously inconsistent results.

As a bonus, the anti-corrosive properties of aluminum and stainless steel provide superior protection for the time vehicle if exposed to unexpected harsh environments, such as acid rain,

ENGINE COVER COMPONENTS

1. NUCLEAR REACTOR
2. STEAM TURBINES
3. REACTOR POWER COILS
4. REACTOR COOLING VENTS
5. RADIATION SCRUBBER VENT
6. HEAT EXCHANGER VENT
7. SIGNAL AMPLIFIER/DRIVER
8. TEMPORAL FIELD GYROSCOPE WITH ANTI-VIBRATION MOUNT
9. COOLANT PUMP
10. HEAT EXCHANGER
11. COOLING SYSTEMS CONTROL UNIT
12. FLUX CAPACITOR EXHAUST DUCT
13. STEAM SEPARATORS
14. PRESSURE EQUALIZER
15. TURBINE COOLANT
16. PRIMARY HYDRAULIC HOSES
17. COOLANT RETURN
18. PUMP CONTROL WIRES
19. STEAM RELEASE
20. HYDRAULIC VENT CONTROL A
21. COOLANT RECLAMATION
22. FLOW CONTROL
23. STEAM SEPARATORS COOLANT
24. POWER CABLES TO PAC COILS
25. HYDRAULIC VENT CONTROL HOSE B

which could become a serious environmental danger in the future.

The aluminum engine cover and emergency cooling vents also act like a massive heat sink, working collectively with the other cooling systems to remove and disperse excess heat from the critical systems, as well as properly venting the Porsche 928 engine.

The fuel tank access is located under the front hood. Later model DeLoreans incorporated a "gas flap" in the hood, making it unnecessary to open the hood to fill the tank. Having an exterior gas flap might be more convenient, but the solid hood provides a seamless surface for the temporal field.

Additionally, each wheel is independently outfitted with its own 500 amp generator, which feeds and charges the particle accelerator power coils and emergency nuclear cooling system.

Upgrading to a customized rear-mount, rear-wheel drive prototype Porsche 928 V8 engine provided true sports car performance. With all of the hardware on board, reaching 88 mph with the stock Volvo engine would have been a struggle, making it virtually impossible to achieve a temporal event.

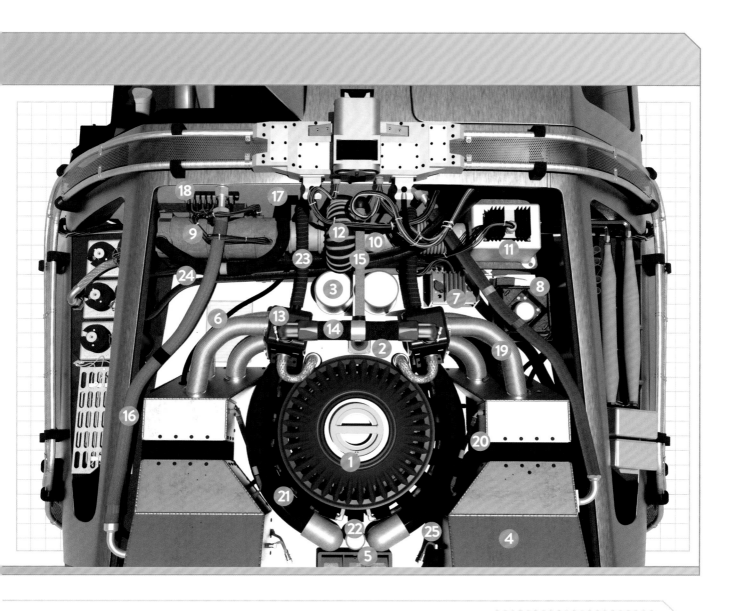

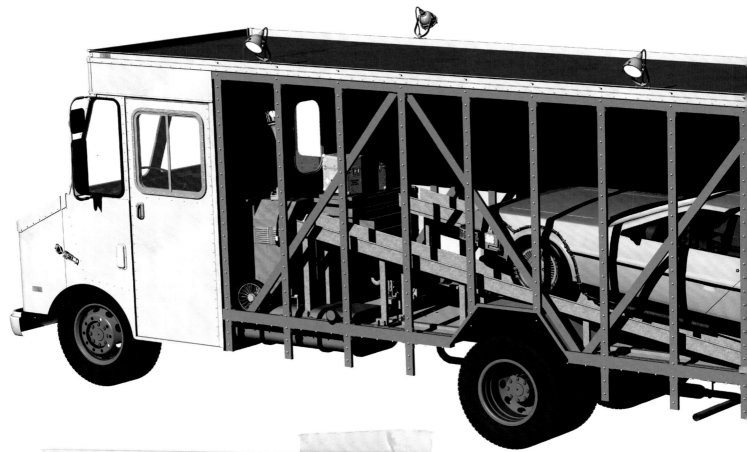

INTERIOR

1. **CASE OF PLUTONIUM**
2. **LINCOLN ARC WELDER**
3. **ARGON GAS CYLINDER**
4. **TOOL CHEST**
5. **REAR GATE & RAMP WINCH**
6. **DELOREAN WINCH**

May 18, 1984

With the purchase of the DeLorean, I modified my GMC P60 Value "Step" van work truck with an automatic folding door/ramp at the rear, so that I could transport the vehicle between my two labs. I also equipped the van with tools and supplies required to perform on-site repairs to the time vehicle.

During transport, when the doors of the DeLorean are sealed, the cabin is automatically pressurized with a mixture of nitrogen and oxygen, vented from the Torin blower on the bulkhead. When the conditions are right, it causes a theatrical display of cloud vapor in the cabin. I'm certain it was a spectacular first sighting of the DeLorean for Marty when he arrived in the parking lot of Twin Pines Mall to assist me with Temporal Experiment number one!

OUTSIDE OF PLUTONIUM, the only 20th century power source capable of generating the necessary 1.21 gigawatts of electricity is a bolt of lightning. In order to allow a lightning rod to channel this electrical energy into the flux capacitor, this assembly is designed to hold a custom-made rod and hook in a stable position. The internal receptacle bypasses the nuclear reactor but ties into the reactor's electrical output, ensuring that the reactor will remain in perfect working order for subsequent time traveling when powered by plutonium instead of lightning. The horizontal stack of current transformers on the exterior assembly are used to accurately measure currents of enormous magnitude.

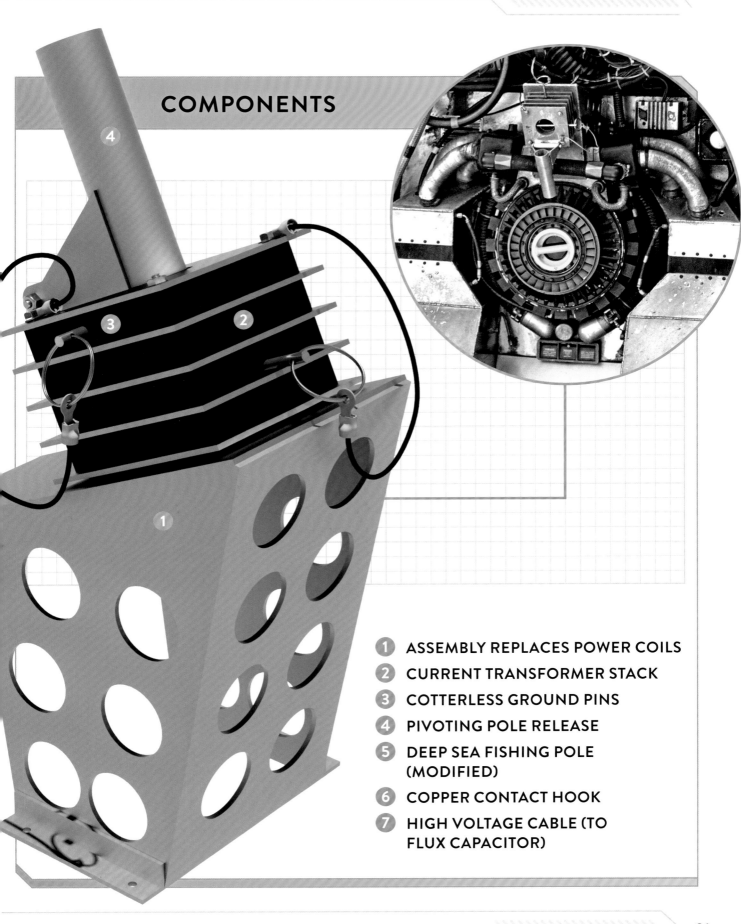

COMPONENTS

1. ASSEMBLY REPLACES POWER COILS
2. CURRENT TRANSFORMER STACK
3. COTTERLESS GROUND PINS
4. PIVOTING POLE RELEASE
5. DEEP SEA FISHING POLE (MODIFIED)
6. COPPER CONTACT HOOK
7. HIGH VOLTAGE CABLE (TO FLUX CAPACITOR)

DOC BROWN'S JOURNALS
2015

November 5, 2015

Science is rife with unusual accidents and, by a strange twist of fate, on October 26, 1985, my assistant Marty McFly inadvertently became the world's first human time traveler, accidentally finding himself stuck in Hill Valley on the day in 1955 that I invented time travel. This was fortuitous in that Marty literally saved my life, as I would have otherwise been shot dead at Twin Pines Mall by Achmed and an unsavory associate. Marty's written warning to me in 1955 had inspired me to acquire a bulletproof vest, and so the Libyans' gunfire only stunned me, knocking me to the pavement.

Upon reviving, I was momentarily dazed as images and impressions flooded my mind. I soon realized that I now had memories in my head of two different histories: one in which Marty had visited me in 1955 and had given me the warning letter, and one in which that had never occurred and I had been murdered. Certainly, no physicist (or philosopher) could have predicted a "multiplicity memory" phenomenon, because no one had ever experienced time travel. Or had they? Is the experience of déjà vu actually the time continuum being revised and reorganized, causing people to "remember" things they can't explain?

With faithful Einstein by my side and the ten remaining plutonium canisters now packed in the trunk, I took Marty home, doing my best to conceal my rising excitement at the prospect of at last traveling into the future—30 years into the future.

It seemed appropriate to choose November 5 as my arrival date—the perfect way to celebrate the 60th anniversary of the breakthrough that led to the invention of the Flux Capacitor. I was unconcerned that the appearance of a 33-year-old car in the year 2015 would create much of a stir, no more than seeing cars from the 1950s in 1985 warranted more than a passing smile. Thus, I made a quick U-turn, accelerated to 88 mph, and I was off!

November 5, 2015, afternoon

Marty was right. Reentry was indeed a little bumpy, although the trip didn't faze Einstein. No matter—we had arrived! Einstein and I were in the future!

And yet, despite confirmation from my time displays, my first impressions led me to believe otherwise. These impressions were, to put it mildly, a shock. As far as I could see, little had changed, at least at my arrival point. It seemed I was still in the 1980s. The cars were the same, and the people were dressed no differently than in 1985. Had I really traveled 30 years into the future to a world in which progress had stagnated? Or had the time circuitry somehow failed and sent me only a year or two ahead?

Within moments, I realized I had arrived in the middle of a 1980s car exposition. The appearance of my 1981 DeLorean, heralded by sonic booms, drew the immediate attention of the crowd—as well as their adulation. In short order, I was regarded as a bit of a hero—not for having traveled through time, but for having a beautiful, customized stainless steel car, the likes of which no one had seen in quite some time.

Things happened so quickly. I was in a sort of daze as people swarmed me and the vehicle to get a good look. Einstein was greeted with joy as well, and I was comforted to know that mankind's love of the faithful canine species had, if anything, only grown. One thing became evident: Cameras had gotten much smaller, and they no longer seemed to require film.

My next clear memory was standing on the dais with the judges at the car expo and winning the first place prize, presented to me by Goldie Wilson III, the grandson of Hill Valley's 1985 mayor, who specialized in hover-converting old automobiles. Young Wilson was the spitting image of his grandfather, minus the gold tooth. And my prize? Ten percent off the cost of a hover conversion at Wilson's auto shop! A hover conversion! Great Scott! By 2015, flying cars, a technological dream for a century, were now a reality!

Young Wilson possessed all of the gregariousness of his grandfather, informing me that the cost of the hover conversion, including federal, state, and local taxes, plus fees from the still despised Department of Motor Vehicles (some things never change), would amount to over $50,000, even with my discount. Plus the additional cost of a "fusion power unit," which I assumed would be significant. I assured him he would be seeing me soon, even though this was a magnitude of money far beyond what I possessed. Clearly, there were financial matters to address, which, in my haste to travel, I had failed to consider.

Einstein and I made our way to the town square. Now <u>this</u> was the future! It was truly incredible! The dilapidated 1985 town square had been redeveloped into what might have been considered a theme park 30 years earlier. Not only were there flying cars, but there

were also low-flying devices similar to small satellites that I learned were called "drones." Advances in health, fitness, and medical technology meant people would live longer—there had been revolutions in almost all walks of life. Volumes could be (and I suppose have been) written, so I shall merely include a single image of this wondrous place.

I will digress to note that the maglev technology that was being pioneered in the 1980s had borne fruit, particularly in the future equivalent of the skateboard, called "hoverboards." In fact, I was so busy looking up at the drones and flying cars that I was knocked down by a youth with a painted face who was "riding" one. Rather than show any concern toward my well-being, he called me a "bojo" and an "old trunkhead," and disappeared around a corner.

And yet, as I marveled at all of this incredible technology, I again wondered... Was this <u>THE</u> future or simply a <u>POSSIBLE</u> future, extrapolated from the particular version of 1985 I had come from? I knew there were at least two versions of 1985, one in which I had been murdered by the Libyans and one in which I had survived. Did these timelines coexist as "alternate dimensions," or was there actually just one single timeline that was being constantly revised and rewritten—just as a river constantly changes course due to environmental variations, with each change in course erasing its previous form?

To me, this "river" analogy made intrinsic sense as it was compatible with what I had already experienced. It meant that time was malleable, that nothing was "written" or preordained, and it allowed for the existence of free will. Hence, the version of 2015 that I was experiencing would be the "real" future until it was rewritten.

Fig 1. Time as the current of a river flows from the past to the future.

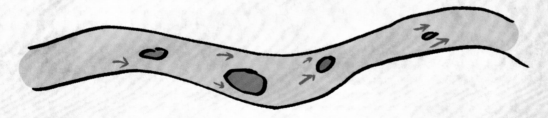

Fig 2. A time traveler could create minor disruptions, the equivalent of stones, that briefly affect and divert the current, but the overall course of the river remains the same.

Fig 3. However, a major disruption, such as the assassination of Adolf Hitler, would be equivalent to a landslide depositing a huge boulder midstream that would completely divert the flow, resulting in a new course for the river of time. The old course (dotted lines) would soon dry up and be erased from existence.

85

So now I had to face a reality of all human societies—money. I had brought a supply of silver dollars with me, knowing that their silver content would be of value, but with high hopes that coin collecting would continue to be enjoyed in the future, and that these specific coins might fetch a significant price. Sadly, not being a numismatist myself, my coins, (some family heirlooms and others left over from a trip to Vegas), were not pristine. My used 1937 coin was worth only nine dollars, and the entire collection, including the family heirlooms, would fetch only $6,300 at the local coin shop.

I visited an antique shop in the town square called "Blast from the Past" to determine if items from 1985 or earlier had escalated in value. But alas, the expensive high-tech items of my day were nothing more than novelty items in 2015. The floppy discs and VHS tapes of 1985 no longer existed, so the devices that utilized them were no better than door stops.

Clearly, the financial situation was going to require some research. I was happy to discover that the Hill Valley Public Library still existed, and I was certain that a librarian would be able to help me. Wonder of wonders, libraries now had computers, vastly improved from the IBM PS/1 and Apple 11 models that existed in 1985. Even more fascinating was something called "internet," by which information from all over the world could be easily accessed.

After some trial and error, I learned how to "surf," to use the colloquialism. But what would my approach be? Although I could travel to the past and invest in some stocks, cashing them in years in the future might create problems, given tax issues and the level of red tape that seemed to have become even more labyrinthine in this new age. And given the rate of inflation, United States Savings Bonds were money losers. Better to buy gold, jewelry, or other tangible objects in the past at a low price to sell for a substantial return in the future. But what "tangible object" would be optimal? I was soon amazed to discover that the single

most profitable item of the past 75 years could be found in 1938 at a price I could easily afford.

I cashed in enough silver dollars to buy appropriate clothes for that period, and before long, I traveled back in time to Hill Valley, arriving on May 25, 1938, a time period which I remembered quite clearly from my youth.

May 25, 1938

I had timed my arrival perfectly. The owner of the newsstand was taking items off the racks that hadn't sold, so—safe in the knowledge that I would not be depriving any child of what was destined to be the most valuable collector's item in history—I used my 1937 silver dollar to purchase the dealer's last ten copies of Action Comics #1, which features the debut of Superman, explaining to the puzzled dealer that I had a lot of grandchildren.

Action Comics #1 ™ & © DC. Used with Permission.

November 12, 2015

$2,500,000! In cash! For just one copy! Truly, the greatest ten-cent investment in history! The auction house had offered me $300,000 more by wire transfer, but without a 2015 bank account or proper credentials, I decided to accept a lesser amount in cash rather than face more questions. Perhaps Mr. Clark of the auction house assumed I was involved in some questionable activities, but a collector's greed usually conquers all, and I know Mr. Clark happily believed he cheated me on the deal. Regardless, I was now financially flush and able to purchase whatever I needed in this timeline. Needing a new 2015 identity, my first task was to buy futuristic clothes.

 I checked into a dog-friendly residence hotel as a base of operations. After establishing credentials for myself in this era, I disconnected the time circuits and flux capacitor in preparation to upgrade the Time Vehicle with every conceivable "bell and whistle" of this amazing future.

 The device known as "Mr. Fusion" was a godsend. It meant I would no longer need to power time travel with plutonium. The 1.25 gigawatt unit I purchased was ten times more powerful than what was needed for a typical automotive hover conversion, or even a rock concert, but I explained that I might be using it for auxiliary power in an industrial situation. The salesman didn't care because he was making more money on the sale, so everyone was happy.

 Now I was ready to visit the hover conversion business operated by Goldie Wilson III.

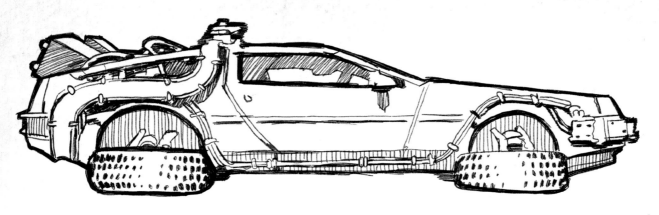

Given the financial issues I had just dealt with, and knowing the truth behind the cliché "money talks," I decided to create a "cash stash" so that I would have appropriate currency for diverse time periods. For now, I focused solely on US Currency.

I was feeling aches and pains from the hoverboard collision, so my next order of business was my own health maintenance. Since money was no object, I again opted for the proverbial "whole nine yards," with a physical overhaul that included a blood cleaning; DNA, epidermis, and hair repair; orthopedic strengthening; a replacement of my spleen and colon; and other processes I quite frankly did not understand. The end result was that I added a good 30 years to my life.

It was after this procedure that I saw a newspaper headline in the Hill Valley edition of "USA Today," which came as a total shock.

The young lady pictured in the story looked like a female version of Marty—no coincidence, since she was his daughter! And her crime was attempting to break her twin brother, Martin McFly Junior, out of prison! Clearly, things had not gone well for my friend, now 47 years old. He had apparently turned out to be less than a good parent. Before attempting any contact with Marty Senior, I decided another research trip to the library was in order.

MARLENE MCFLY REPORTS TO SAN QUENTIN

(Nov. 12, San Quentin) Marlene McFly, daughter of Martin and Jennifer McFly of Hilldale, reported to San Quentin Prison today to begin her 20-year sentence for attempting to break her brother, Martin McFly Jr, out of Hill County lockup on October 31. Martin Jr. had been awaiting transfer to Folsom Prison for his part in the failed October 23 payroll robbery of Vandesco Industries.

His sister used a false ID in an attempt to hijack the transfer vehicle, but her ruse was discovered due to suspicious biometrics. Marlene McFly was convicted of several offenses, including fraud with intent to commit a felony, use of a false ID, identity theft, and trespassing. Her devastated parents accompanied her to San Quentin and bid her a tearful farewell. She will be eligible for parole in 2022.

LOCAL YOUTH INJURED IN DRAG RACE

(Oct. 28, Hill Valley) A daylight drag race resulted in tragedy for a Hill Valley High School student, although the outcome could have been far worse. Martin McFly, 17, suffered a broken right arm, a crushed right hand, and a minor concussion after his black Toyota pickup truck broadsided a white Rolls Royce near the new Hilldale development on Clayton Road. The driver of the Rolls Royce, business executive Durwood Bennington, suffered only minor bruises but may press charges. McFly refused to name his racing opponent, but, based on eyewitness accounts and descriptions of the vehicle, police believe it was Douglas Needles, 18. McFly is recovering at Hill County Hospital.

Within a few hours, I ascertained that Marty's dream of becoming a rock star had been ended by a hand injury received in an avoidable drag racing accident. Marty ended up in a dead-end job, and Jennifer married him out of pity. His twin progeny, lacking a strong father figure, had become, as Marty would put it, "complete wimps" who made one bad decision after another. Another case of history repeating itself.

I pondered this long and hard. I could easily travel back to 1985 and prevent the fateful drag race. But the incident was caused by Marty's own hot-headedness, a character flaw that would inevitably get him into some other trouble later, perhaps at the cost of his life. I did not possess the tools that would allow Marty to keep his head whenever he was called "chicken." Yet, I was troubled that his relatively innocent offspring were paying the price for their father's irresponsibility. Despite the Bible's admonition that the sins of the father would be visited on the children, I wondered if something could be done about those kids.

The incident that had sent Marty Junior to prison occurred on October 21, 2015, and involved a particularly nasty character named Griff.

If *that* incident could be prevented, Marty Junior would not go to jail, and perhaps he and his sister would have a chance to improve themselves. And given Marty Junior's striking resemblance to his father at that age, an idea began to crystallize. I would travel back to that fateful day and, using the current state-of-the-art spy technology, learn exactly what had happened. I decided to place Einstein in a kennel so that I could develop my plan without distractions. Because my plan would necessitate bringing the Marty of 1985 here to 2015, it was best not to burden my canine compadre with unnecessary time travel, and were something to go wrong, I had to make sure he would be cared for...

YOUTH JAILED
Martin McFly Junior Arrested for Theft

Youth Gang Denies Complicity

By Compu-Fax, USA TODAY

Protesting that he was "put up to the whole thing" by a local gang, Martin McFly, Junior, 17, was arrested for the theft of an undisclosed cash amount by Hill Valley Police this morning. The theft, which was accomplished with a stolen degaussing unit, took place at the Hill Valley Payroll Substation on 9th Street at exactly 1:28 A.M. this morning. Police were sketchy about details, but apparently McFly setoff a pressure sensitive alarm system which alerted authorities. McFly, the son of Martin and Jennifer McFly of Hilldale. accused members of a local gang of putting him up to the crime. Griff Tannen, spokesman for the accused youths, denied any involvement. "McFly's too low-res for us to associate with him,"

McFly insisted that the gang was involved and that he didn't even know that he was committing a crime. "They told me it was simply a money making opportunity, and that it was entirely legal."

McFly will be arraigned tomorrow and will be tried in a data-fax court later this week.

The McFly family is no stranger to run-ins with the law. Martin McFly was involved in a drag racing accident involving an innocent bystander in 1985.

Martin McFly, Junior: "They made me do it."

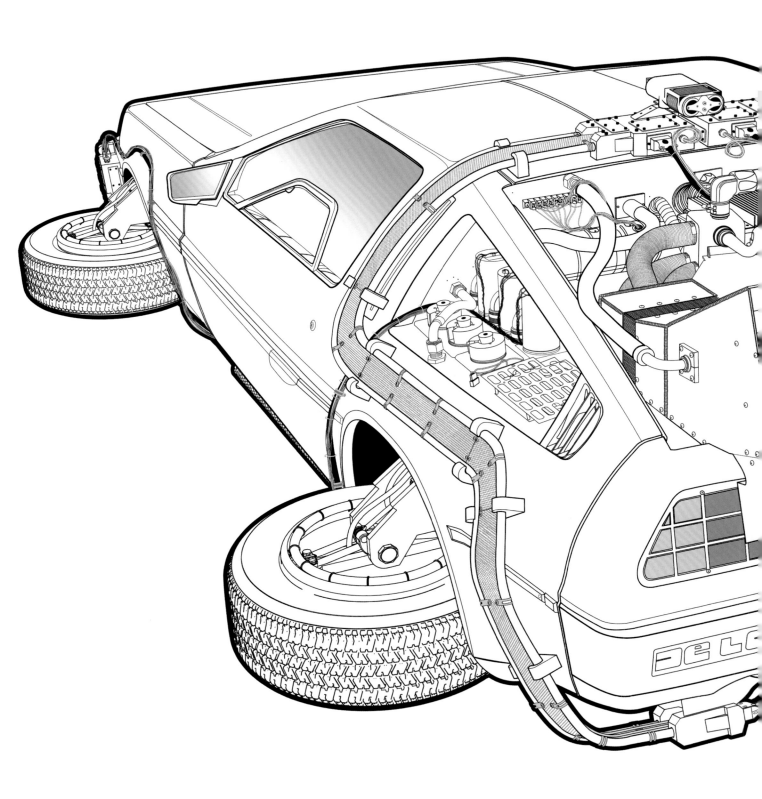

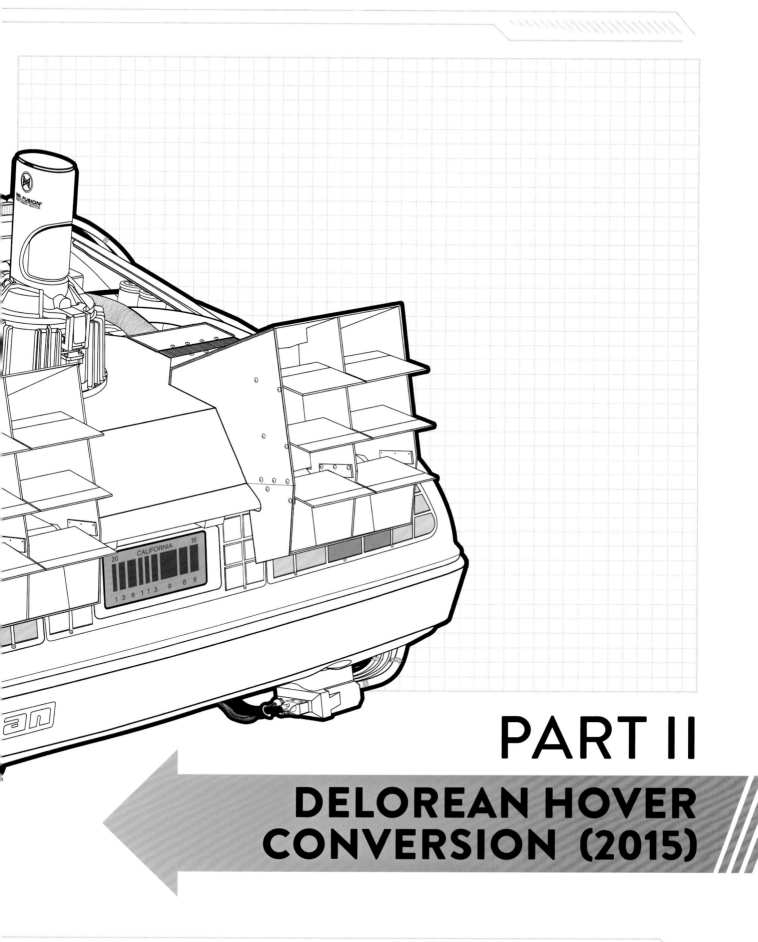

PART II

DELOREAN HOVER CONVERSION (2015)

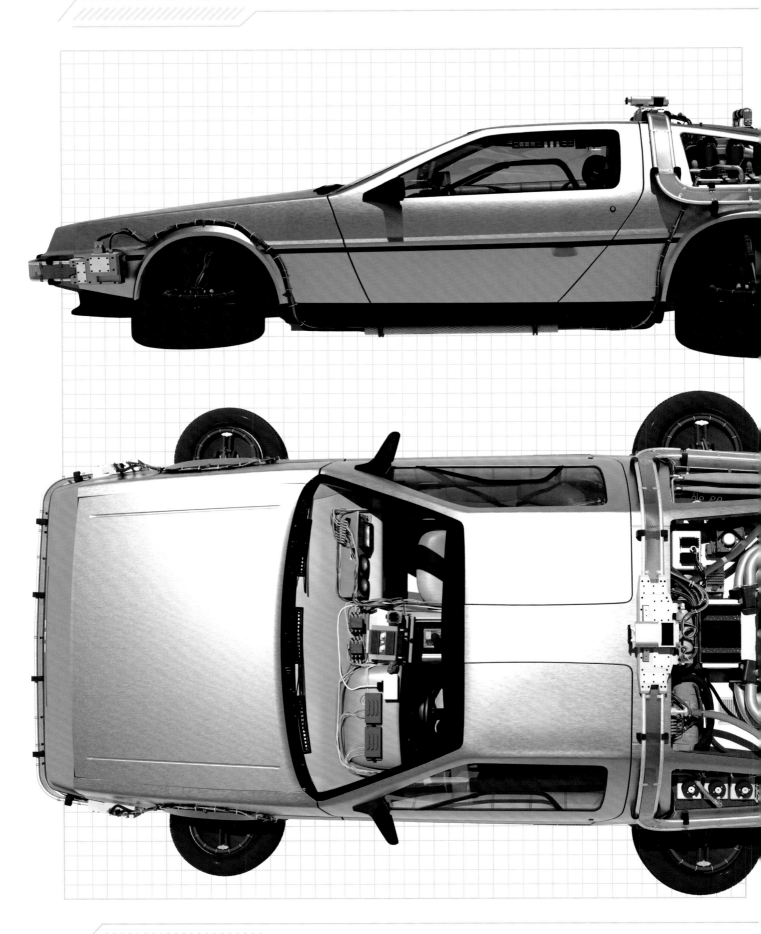

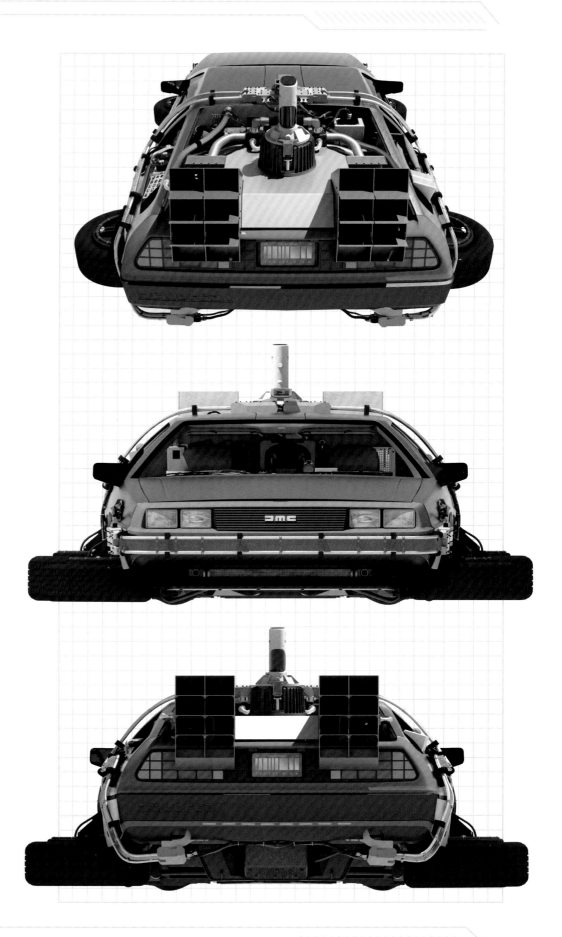

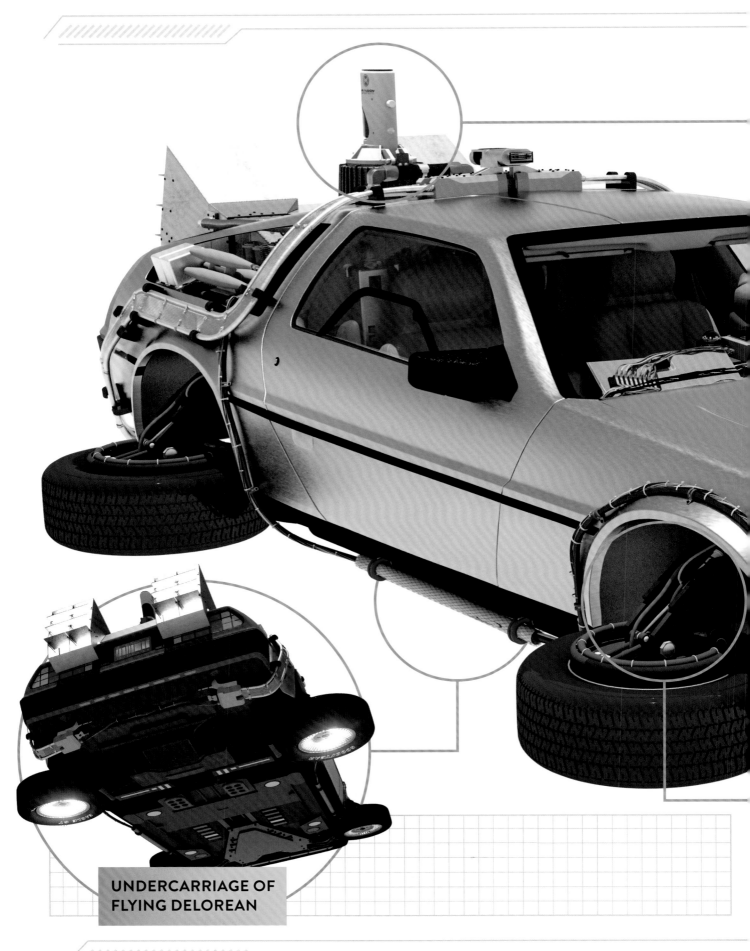

UNDERCARRIAGE OF
FLYING DELOREAN

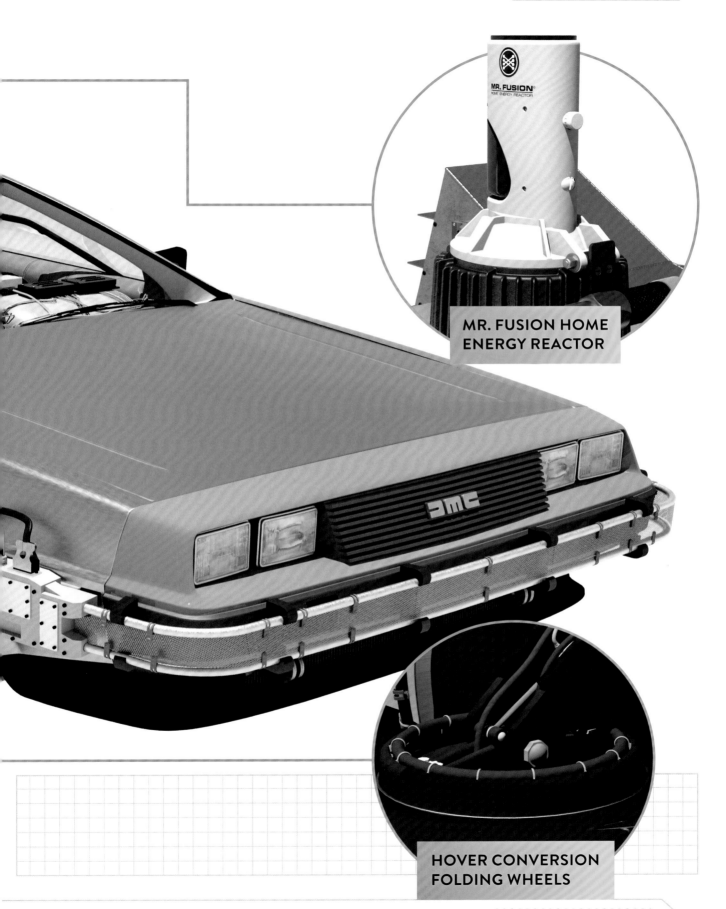

MR. FUSION HOME
ENERGY REACTOR

HOVER CONVERSION
FOLDING WHEELS

MR. FUSION

In the future, I would install the Mr. Fusion energy reactor, allowing me to tap into a virtually endless source of power for the flux capacitor and other temporal components as well as the hover conversion systems. However, gasoline would always be required to run the car's internal combustion engine.

QUARTER VIEW

TOP VIEW

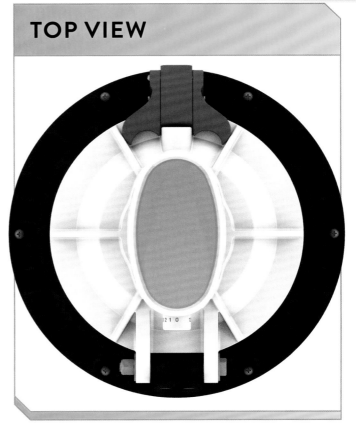

FIG. 1.

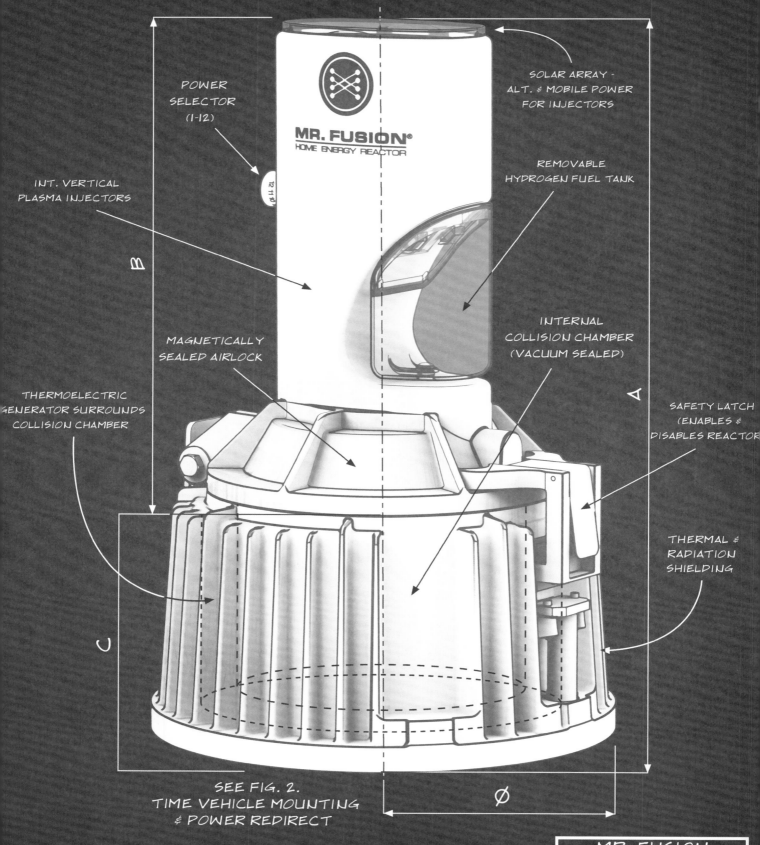

POWER
SELECTOR
(1-12)

SOLAR ARRAY -
ALT. & MOBILE POWER
FOR INJECTORS

INT. VERTICAL
PLASMA INJECTORS

REMOVABLE
HYDROGEN FUEL TANK

MR. FUSION®
HOME ENERGY REACTOR

B

MAGNETICALLY
SEALED AIRLOCK

INTERNAL
COLLISION CHAMBER
(VACUUM SEALED)

A

THERMOELECTRIC
GENERATOR SURROUNDS
COLLISION CHAMBER

SAFETY LATCH
(ENABLES &
DISABLES REACTOR)

THERMAL &
RADIATION
SHIELDING

C

SEE FIG. 2.
TIME VEHICLE MOUNTING
& POWER REDIRECT

Ø

HR2015FC-3

Ø	A	B	C
5.8125"	18.25"	12.125"	6.125"
147.6375MM	463.55MM	307.975MM	155.58MM

MR. FUSION
REACTOR

REPLACEMENT FOR
NUCLEAR REACTOR

FULL SCALE
CONFIDENTIAL

DRAWN BY:
E. Brown
DATE: 09/08/2015

FIG. 2.

MR. FUSION
REACTOR
REPLACEMENT FOR
NUCLEAR REACTOR
FULL SCALE
CONFIDENTIAL
DRAWN BY: E. Brown
DATE: 09 / 08 / 2015

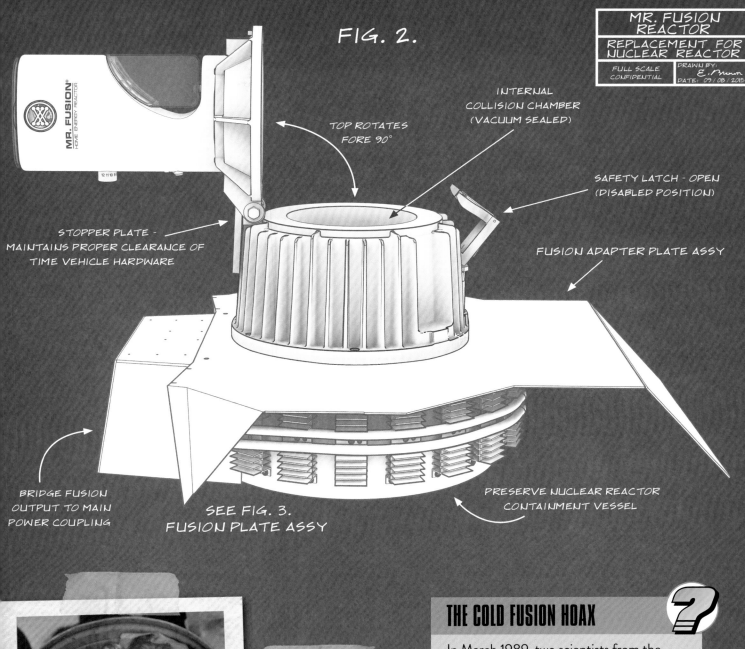

INTERNAL
COLLISION CHAMBER
(VACUUM SEALED)

TOP ROTATES
FORE 90°

SAFETY LATCH - OPEN
(DISABLED POSITION)

STOPPER PLATE -
MAINTAINS PROPER CLEARANCE OF
TIME VEHICLE HARDWARE

FUSION ADAPTER PLATE ASSY

BRIDGE FUSION
OUTPUT TO MAIN
POWER COUPLING

SEE FIG. 3.
FUSION PLATE ASSY

PRESERVE NUCLEAR REACTOR
CONTAINMENT VESSEL

THE COLD FUSION HOAX

In March 1989, two scientists from the University of Utah claimed to have solved one of the great problems in physics by perfecting cold fusion. If true, their discovery promised unlimited energy for the world. They were celebrities for a few months until no other scientist in the world was able to duplicate their results. Further examination of their techniques revealed shoddy procedures. Their claim was deemed a hoax, and they were shunned by the scientific community ever after. Cold fusion continues to be an elusive holy grail of physics, more fiction than fact.

HOVERBOARDS

EXTERNAL COMPONENTS

IN THE EARLY 21st century, a team of scientists developed a system combining the principles of magnetic levitation (maglev) and superconductivity along with new proprietary technology to create levitation via ultrathin induction coils and core hyper-magnets that utilize the Earth's magnetic field in conjunction with the grounding properties of the planet's surface and rapid polarity switching. The technology turned out to be limited in scale, capable of levitating a maximum weight of 125 kg (275 pounds) about 8 cm (3.5 inches). With industrial applications limited, the technology was instead used to create skateboards without wheels, known as "hoverboards." Hoverboards proved immensely popular with young people. Much to the chagrin of surfers, the technology did not work over water, which disrupted the magnetic fields.

INTERNAL COMPONENTS

1. SUPERCONDUCTING CERAMIC RING
2. ROTATIONAL SPEED OF 5000 RPM
3. LIQUID NITROGEN COOLANT CHAMBER
4. HIGH TENSILE PLATE (HOUSES EACH HYPER-MAGNET)
5. EIGHT CARBON FIBER STRUTS (MAINTAIN RING INTEGRITY)
6. SOLENOIDS (CREATE MAGNETIC FIELDS AROUND RIM)

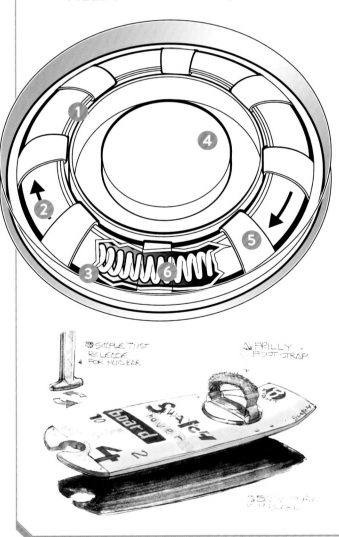

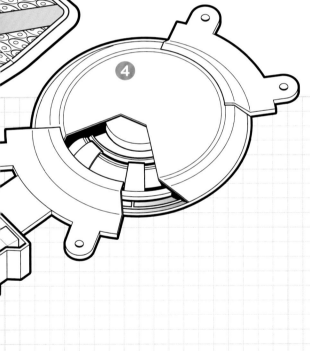

1. VELOCITY CONTROL PADS
2. SAFETY STRAP
3. POLARITY REVERSING ACCELERATION BOOSTER
4. CIRCULAR HOUSING (PROTECTS INTERNAL COMPONENTS)

CONCEPT DESIGNS

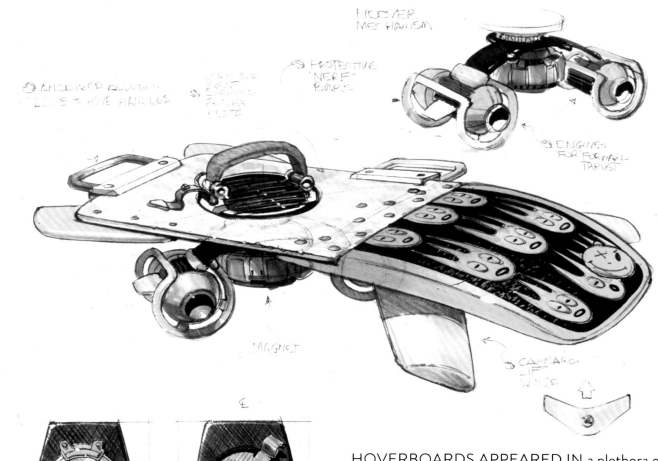

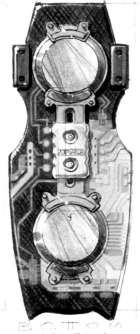

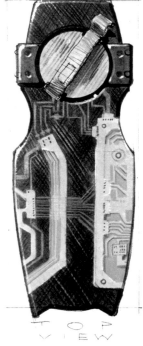

HOVERBOARDS APPEARED IN a plethora of designs, including scooter versions for very young children. Hoverboarding competitions became one of the most popular extreme sports, with champion hoverboarders winning prizes in excess of one million dollars. The popularity of hoverboards also helped curb obesity in young people because no teenager wanted to be "too heavy to hover." Small but powerful engines became available as add-ons, providing a burst of power that could propel a hoverboard over a pond or river.

The workings of a typical hoverboard include two magnetic plates that house the twin hyper-magnets. They are connected via lengthy coils, wound in similar fashion to the wire in electromagnets. Proprietary technology, in the form of silicon and ceramic chips and capacitance circuitry, is usually contained in the housings that frame the magnetic plates.

DOC BROWN'S JOURNALS
1885

November 12, 1955 / January 1, 1885

There's an old saying: "If you want to make God laugh, tell Him your plans." God must certainly be laughing after my ill-fated decision to save Marty's children. I had invited Marty and his girlfriend, Jennifer, into the Time Machine and brought them both to the year 2015. My overt paranoia about Jennifer seeing the Time Machine led to the systematic unraveling of my plan. For now, suffice it to say that the resulting events—which involved the theft of the time vehicle and a sports almanac by the nefarious Biff Tannen—proved my "river" theory of time, the flow of which, we discovered upon returning to 1985, had been diverted, leading to a hellish version of Hill Valley dominated by the middle-aged Biff. In a subsequent trip to November 12, 1955, Marty successfully repaired the timeline. But no one could have predicted what occurred next.

While attempting to safely land and pick up Marty in 1955, the time vehicle was, ironically, struck by a bolt of lightning, which sent over 1.21 gigawatts of electrical energy into the flux capacitor. Although the vehicle was traveling at less than 88 miles per hour, the impact point of the lightning bolt sent the vehicle into a sudden rotation, which I assume must have reached that speed. Marty, watching from the ground, would have seen the fire trails as spirals, looking like the number 99. Due to a glitch in the time circuits, which I had actually noticed earlier, the destination time had become set to January 1, 1885. And that's where I ended up. Fortunately, I somehow managed to land upright, badly shaken but unharmed, at least physically. But the devastating sense of depression and guilt that engulfed me

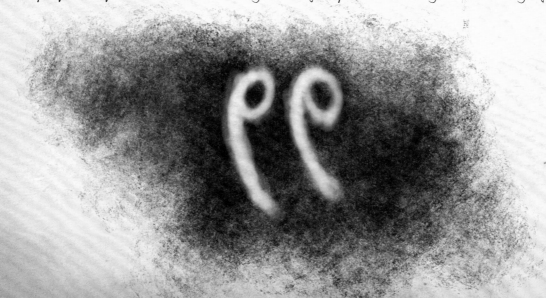

was far greater than how I'd felt observing the dystopian 1985 that Marty and I had just repaired. There, we had at least been together. Now, my best friend was stranded in 1955, while my 2nd best friend, my dog, Einstein, was without companionship in 1985—and it was all my fault.

I surveyed the damage. My worst fears were confirmed: The lightning bolt had fried both the flying circuits and the time circuits. I knew that there would be no way to repair either system using 1885 technology.

I was stuck, and so was Marty, at least until I could figure something out. Even if it took years, my primary objective was now the rescue of my friend. It was my hope that I would eventually devise a course of action that would minimize the enormity of his plight. If I failed, I suppose the worst-case scenario would be that he would become a rock-and-roll star in the 1950s by playing songs that he knew would be hits in the future. But this was a flight of fancy that I did not need to take, certainly not now.

The young town of Hill Valley was a good two miles away, and I was in the wilderness, with little likelihood of anyone coming by. But why take chances? The vehicle was still drivable, so I maneuvered it into a gully and covered it with brush. It would, I hoped, be safe for at least 48 hours and, with the wheels locked, there would be little chance of anyone getting it out even if it was discovered. My foresight in acquiring appropriate currency gave me some satisfaction, and I took solace in knowing that I was in a reasonably civilized time period, as opposed to Hill Valley in the year 1200. The Old West of California was a romantic period, at least in my imagination, even though intellectually, I knew that 19th-century standards in sanitation and health would shatter some of those youthful fantasies. When I was a child, my father, inspired by the boyhood of young Theodore Roosevelt, sent me away over four or five summers to what is now called "wilderness camp," where I learned to ride horses, hunt, camp, fish, and acquire other outdoor survival skills. Those were some of the most wonderful summers of my youth.

I thoroughly examined my clothing to ensure that I would not stand out upon arriving in town. My overcoat was a godsend, but my hat would have to remain behind. And with enough dirt on my shoes, I doubted they would attract attention. As I made the two-mile trek, I conceived a cover story. I would remain "Emmett Brown"—my own family would not immigrate to Hill Valley until 1908, and they would be the Von Brauns until World War 1, so there was no danger of my running into my ancestors. If asked, I would say that I had come to town hurriedly via horse, after having been falsely accused of hanky-panky in Pine City on New Year's Eve, thus explaining my lack of possessions. My horse didn't make it, and now I was ready to make a fresh start.

The Hill Valley of 1885 was barely recognizable—the foundations for the courthouse had only recently been laid, and there were few businesses that would survive the years. Interestingly, there was a horse trader named Joe Statler whose family would go on to deal in automobiles, and a manure hauler named Abraham Jones, whose family would remain in the cleanup and sanitation business.

February 25, 1885

I've been so busy that I haven't had time to update my journal. My integration into 19th Century Hill Valley has been surprisingly easy. Certainly, having cash has been a significant factor. Fortuitously, the town had been in need of a blacksmith because the previous tradesman, although competent, had a penchant for gambling, and had incurred debts he was unable to pay. He had disappeared right before Christmas, leaving his entire operation behind. Therefore I was able to purchase his shop and all its equipment from his creditors at a discount, as they were more than happy to accept an immediate cash offer. The shop was in a barn facing what would eventually become town square, and it was the perfect cover for me to proceed with further work on the time vehicle. Although I knew my presence might conceivably alter history to a small degree, I believed I could be careful—not that I had a choice. Hiding in solitary was certainly not an option, and I had to make the best of things. Most of all, there was my responsibility to Marty and to Einie.

Within days of procuring the barn, some new clothing, equipment, and two horses, I retrieved the time vehicle and, under cover of night, towed it back to my shop. I took precautions to keep it covered, but on those occasions when a customer spotted it, I simply explained it was new equipment with which I was experimenting.

I made certain to ingratiate myself with the citizenry of Hill Valley. Most important was Marshal James Strickland, who was the future grandfather of Stanford

Strickland, a rather tightly wound classmate of mine who eventually became the principal of the high school. Discipline was clearly a Strickland family tradition. The Marshal was happy to know that the new blacksmith was not a deadbeat. I assured him I was a proponent of law and order, and that my services to him and his deputies would be rendered free of charge. This promise was cheap insurance in the event that one of my experiments went awry and the constabulary was summoned.

April 3, 1885

After three months, my business was thriving. I used future knowledge of metallurgy and welding to repair wagons, tools, and other items for the townspeople. My boyhood experience with horses helped me keep the animals calm during the shoeing process. Indeed, I became so busy that I barely had time to focus on the problem of the Time Machine. I even considered taking on an assistant to lighten the workload, but I realized such a situation could lead to disaster. However, it was a delight becoming a pillar of the community, a significant contrast to my alter ego as a crackpot pariah decades in the future.

Even as I pondered the conundrum of rescuing Marty, I took some personal time to create a few inventions to improve my quality of life.

Wood chopping machine

June 12, 1885

I knew that there was only one man in the world capable of rescuing Marty: me. Or, should I say, the "me" of 1955. Only my younger self could do the necessary repairs to the time vehicle, but he (or should I say "I"? Time travel can make pronouns and tenses difficult) would need detailed instructions. Thus, a two-part plan begun coalescing in my head: Part one involved creating those instructions, and part two involved delivering them. Although advanced micro-circuitry was not feasible in 1955, I recalled that the invention of transistors and chips was motivated by the desire for an effective replacement for the somewhat fragile (and heavy) vacuum tubes that would be "state of the art" 70 years from now. Therefore, I could reverse engineer the time circuits with tubes and rely on my 1955 self to assemble it all. I began devising a schematic...

Map to Time Machine

Approximate scale: One Hundred and sixty-four to one

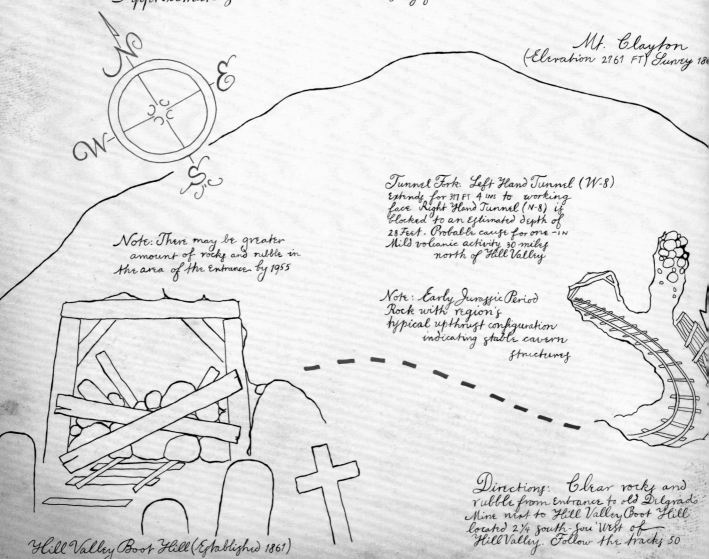

Mt. Clayton
(Elevation 2761 FT) Survey 18

Tunnel Fork: Left Hand Tunnel (W-8)
Extends for 317 FT 4 INS to working
face. Right Hand Tunnel (N-8) is
blocked to an Estimated depth of
28 Feet. Probable cause for one - IN
Mild volcanic activity 30 miles
north of Hill Valley

Note: There may be greater
amount of rocks and rubble in
the area of the Entrance by 1955

Note: Early Jurassic Period
Rock with region's
typical upthrust configuration
indicating stable cavern
structures

Directions: Clear rocks and
rubble from Entrance to old Delgado's
Mine next to Hill Valley Boot Hill
located 2¼ south-sou'west of
Hill Valley. Follow the tracks 50

Hill Valley Boot Hill (Established 1861)

July 23, 1885

Part two of my plan was inspired by Robert Louis Stevenson's "Treasure Island." If I could hide the Time Machine somewhere, effectively "burying" it, and somehow get a corresponding "treasure map" to Marty and myself in 1955, he/we/they could locate it. The next critical question was where to hide the DeLorean in 1885 so that it would survive 70 years untouched and protected from the elements. This required weeks of thought, as I wracked my brain to remember how our town would develop over the next 70 years. It was a news item in the "Hill Valley Telegraph," our local newspaper, that was the catalyst: The Delgado Silver Mine had been played out, and there was nothing to be found in those mine shafts but dirt. It was the perfect solution. I recalled exploring those tunnels as a boy with a few of the neighborhood kids, ignoring the "Danger" and "No Trespassing" signs. Stanford Strickland, always the killjoy, tattled on us. Various parents and police dragged us out of there, and my mother read me the riot act, forbidding me from listening to the radio for an entire week. Therefore, I knew I could hide the time vehicle along with some diagrams in a side shaft, cover it up, and be virtually certain it would remain safely undisturbed until 1955.

Detail of Wall

MARTY ↴

August 10, 1885

I drained all of the fluids from the vehicle to protect it, knowing that equivalent motor oil, brake fluid, and gasoline would be available in 1955. I also knew that the tires would not last 70 years and would undoubtedly disintegrate upon touch when the car was eventually discovered. No matter—rubber tires were plentiful in 1955, too.

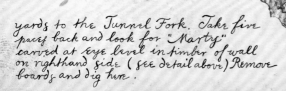

DeLorean is concealed in cavern and covered with animal skins cured in 80% concentrate lye to preserve against damp and dust particles

yards to the Tunnel Fork. Take five paces back and look for "Marty" carved at eye level in timber of wall on righthand side (see detail above) Remove boards and dig here.

August 18, 1885

With the revised time circuit schematic complete, I was ready to hide the vehicle, which I wrapped securely in cloth. Its stainless steel body provided another level of protection. This was more than a one-man job, so I hired a local character named Crazy Ben, who had a penchant for telling wild, unbelievable stories between his drinking binges. No one ever believed a word he said, so I knew my secrets would be safe. Still, as a precautionary measure, I blindfolded him until we arrived at what I had decided was the perfect hiding place in the mine.

I was careful to precisely map the route from the entrance, so that I could transcribe the information into the message I would leave for Marty. And, inspired by Jules Verne's character Arne Saknussemm in "Journey to the Center of the Earth," I carved my initials into support beams along the way to serve as signposts.

August 20, 1885

My positive feelings about how things were proceeding were put on hold when I received a personal visit from the notorious outlaw Buford "Mad Dog" Tannen, who wanted me to shoe his horse.

He had timed his visit to coincide with an out-of-town trip by Marshal Strickland. As much as I wanted to refuse the job, I decided discretion was the better part of valor and agreed to do it. It obviously wouldn't serve the space-time continuum if Tannen went "mad dog" on me and shot me. I promised to have the job done within 2 hours, as I wanted to get him out of my life as quickly as possible. When he returned, he refused to pay me, claiming to be "short of funds at the current time." I had little choice but to tell him to pay me when he next was in town. With Tannen gone, I could again turn to the key problem at hand.

September 1, 1885

The problem: how to ensure that Marty would receive the information at the appropriate time? This was the final piece of the puzzle that I had been mulling over for days. I took my morning constitutional, cogitating over the problem, and happened by the local Western Union office. The company advertised "Your Message Delivered Accurately and Promptly, Guaranteed."

Knowing that Western Union would still be around in Hill Valley in 1955, I realized this could be the answer... assuming I could convince the clerk that I was not out of my mind when I made my request. But I had nothing to lose. I hurried back to my shop and wrote a letter to Marty to be delivered on November 12, 1955, literally right on the highway where he was standing, just moments after I was struck by lightning. I placed both the letter and the map into envelopes, and those into another envelope, sealed with wax to guard against prying eyes. I then put that sealed envelope into a larger package. As I surmised, the clerk thought I was drunk, even though the saloon hadn't opened. I explained my request twice to him and twice more to his boss when he arrived an hour later: "I want this package left with the Hill Valley Western Union office, untouched until November 1955, at which time the package can be opened and the delivery instructions can be read." When the manager questioned my motives, I asked how he could be sure that my inquiry wasn't actually coming from the main corporate headquarters as a test? Did he know what might happen to him if I reported that he refused a customer request? The gentleman not only acquiesced, but he wrote his own set of instructions on the package—which included the words, "by order of the corporate office"— before signing and dating it. Since he was not sure how much to charge for this service, I gave him a twenty dollar gold piece, which he considered more than appropriate.

And now, these matters are out of my hands. All I can do is hope that Western Union is as good as their guarantee. I'm certain that as long as Marty receives the letter, my younger self will be able to get him back to 1985, where he will take care of Einstein. And I can look forward to spending the rest of my years in 19th century Hill Valley as a respectable citizen.

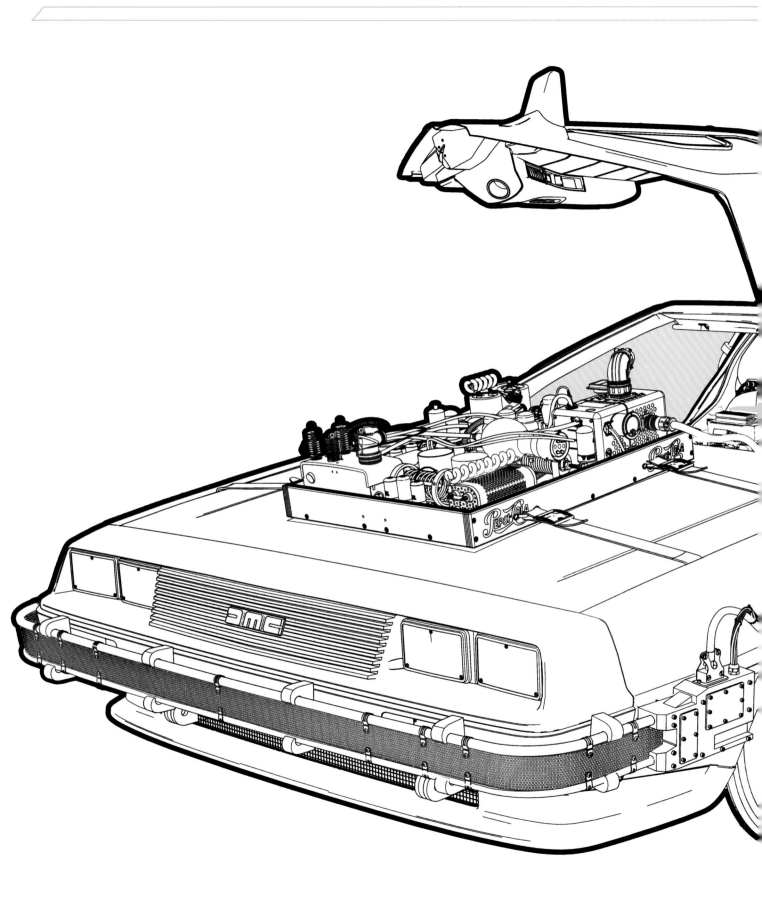

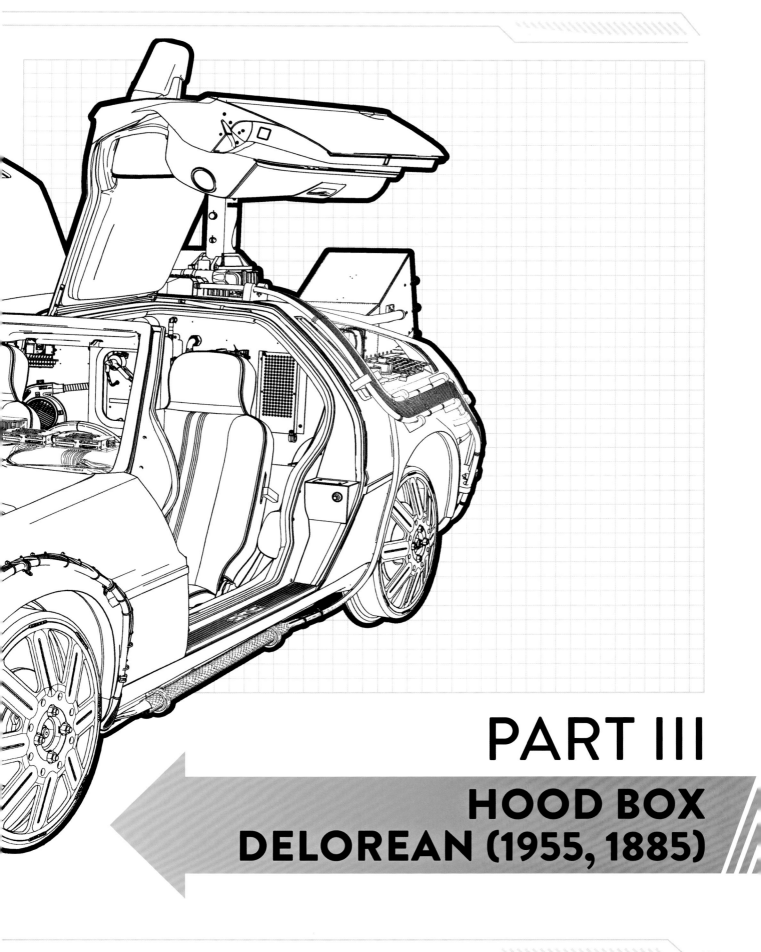

PART III

HOOD BOX
DELOREAN (1955, 1885)

OFF-ROAD DELOREAN

November 15, 1955

My challenge was to send Marty back to September, 1885, to find my older self and prevent his (my) murder at the hands of Buford Tannen, a horrifying event we had uncovered while recovering the vehicle from the mine. After constructing the hoodbox to replace the time circuits, I determined the optimum location for Marty's time travel was the Pohatchee Drive-In Theater. Because the vehicle would be traveling from a flat gravel parking area to the uneven open terrain of Hill Valley, 1885, several modifications were necessary. The suspension and chassis were raised significantly to reduce the possibility of the car bottoming out and ripping apart critical components on the ground. Larger, more durable tires were installed, and the engine and gearing system were retooled. Other adjustments were made in the fuel system to ensure that the leaded gasoline of 1955 would be compatible with a system originally designed for unleaded gasoline. Upon travel to 1885, I also knew that Marty would be grateful for the newly enhanced shock absorbers when navigating the rocky terrain of the Old West.

THE ORIGINAL 1985 Goodyear Eagle GT tires disintegrated after 70 years in the Delgado Mine and were replaced in 1955 by Sears brand F78-14 with $2\frac{3}{8}$-inch whitewalls retreaded by Goodyear with treadwear rated 80 and tread width of 6.26 inches.

DELOREAN OFF-ROAD CAR

THE TIME CIRCUITS MICROCHIP replacement hood component box is secured using maximum strength rawhide belts to withstand the stress and strains of time travel, in terms of both g-forces and temperature.

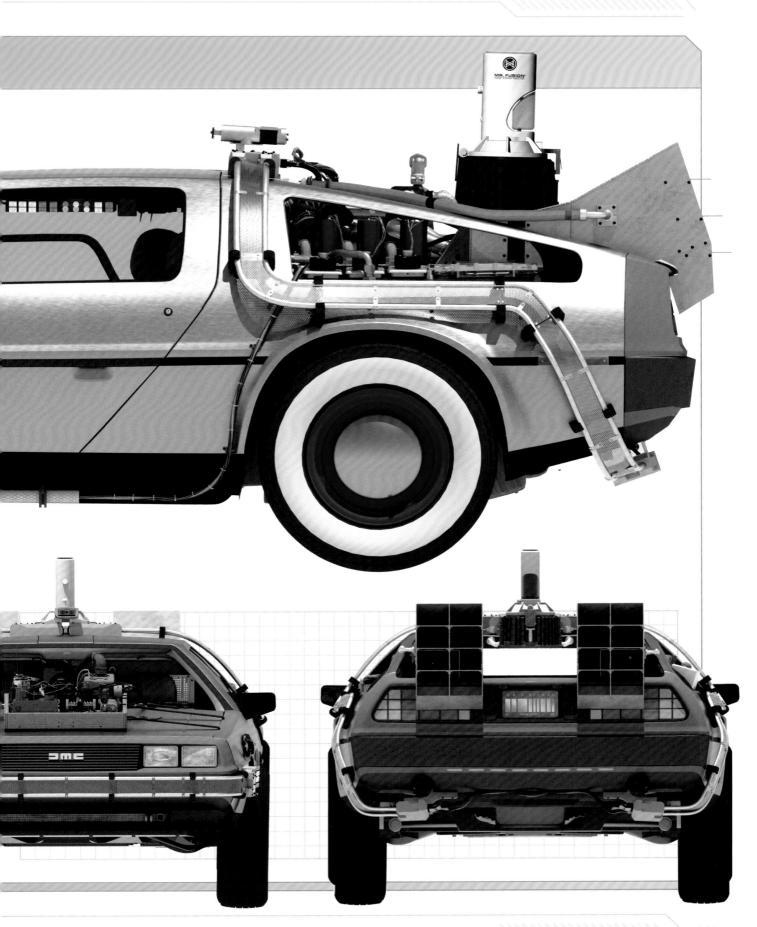

HOOD BOX

HOOD BOX COMPONENTS

1. SOLA CONSTANT VOLTAGE TRANSFORMER
2. ART-13 PA PLATE METER
3. AMPHENOL POWER CONNECTOR
4. CANNON POWER CONNECTOR
5. SHURITE METER
6. CUTLER HAMMER RELAYS
7. GE MOTOR STARTER
8. SPRAGUE CAPACITORS ASSEMBLY
9. VACUUM TUBES (32 ASSORTED)
10. GE EDGEWOUND RESISTOR
11. EIMAC 250TH VACUUM TUBE
12. GE CAGE RESISTOR (TYPE SJO COIL)

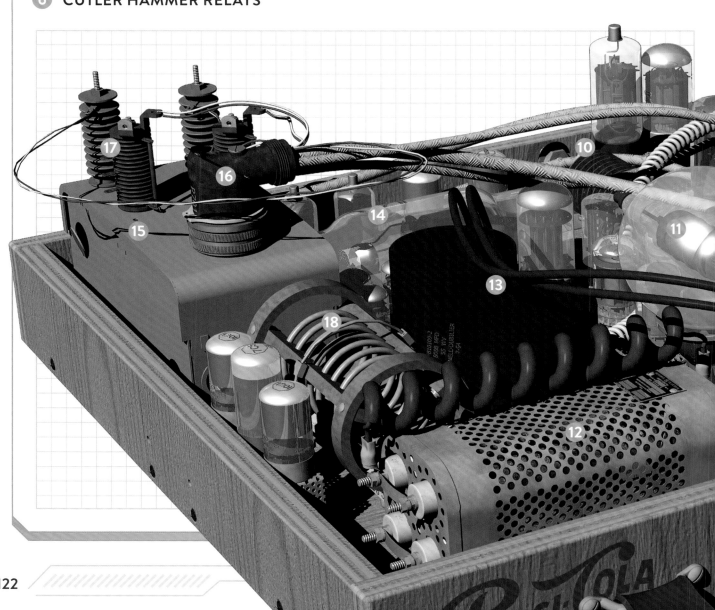

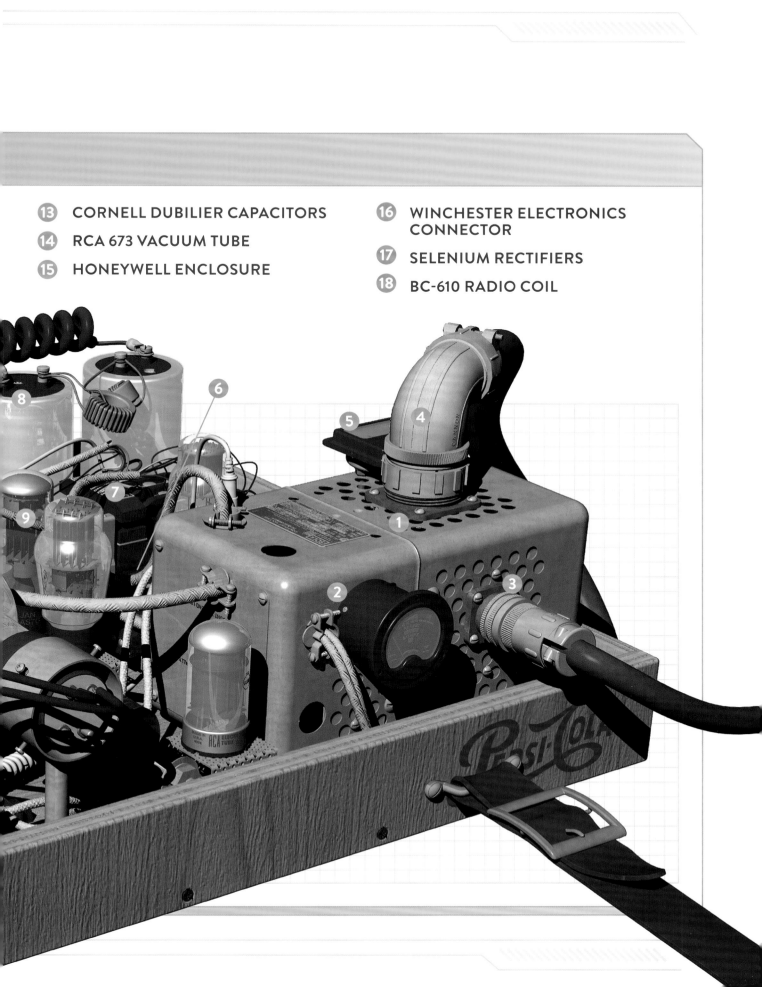

13 CORNELL DUBILIER CAPACITORS

14 RCA 673 VACUUM TUBE

15 HONEYWELL ENCLOSURE

16 WINCHESTER ELECTRONICS CONNECTOR

17 SELENIUM RECTIFIERS

18 BC-610 RADIO COIL

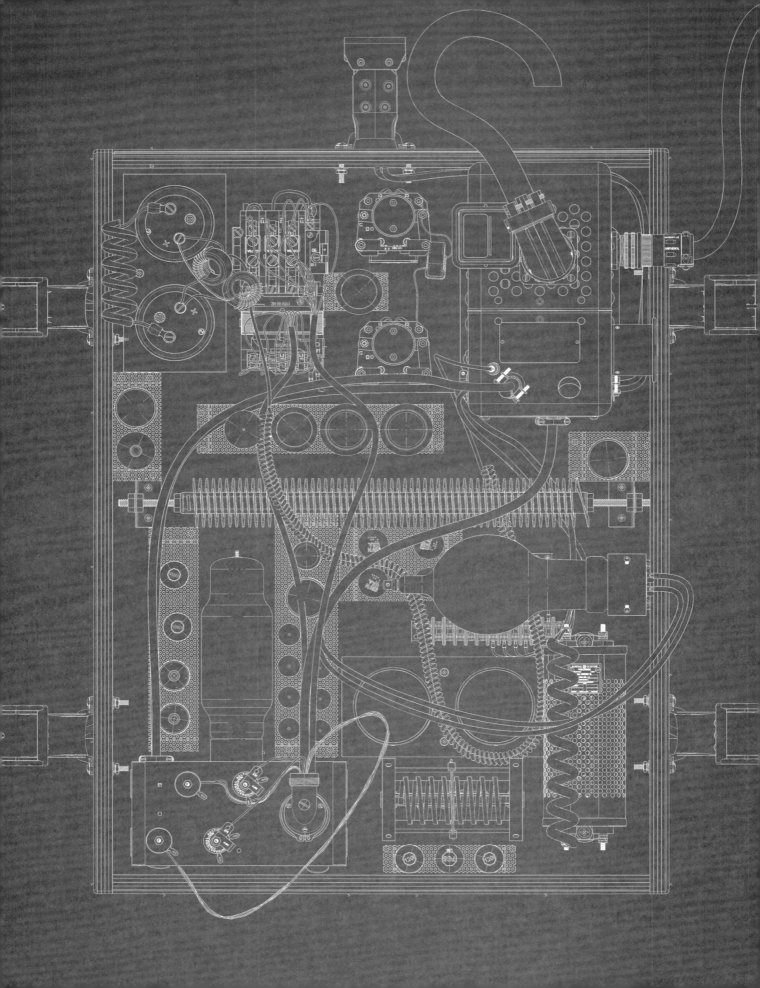

There can be no better image to depict the difference between solid-state chip technology and 20th-century vacuum tube technology than this blueprint and its physical realization of the time circuits control microchip in 1955. The 1955 version is 300 to 400 times the size of the component it has to replace! Although I am a physicist by formal education, my avocation as an inventor required me to learn electrical and mechanical engineering—mostly self-taught, aided by my annual subscriptions to "Popular Mechanics," "Popular Electronics," and other engineering publications. With this knowledge, I was able to create a schematic for my 1955 counterpart that he could convert into a blueprint and construct into a hood box version of the time circuit chip, using parts available in that era. That schematic was carefully placed inside the time vehicle before it was securely wrapped up for its 70-year storage in the Delgado Mine.

September 5, 1885

Despite my precautions, the vehicle's fuel line had ripped and the gas had leaked out upon Marty's arrival in 1885. With no acceptable fuel substitute, the only way to get it up to 88 mph was to have it pushed along train tracks by a steam locomotive, powered by modified "presto logs" that would increase the steam engine's heat and speed. To adapt the time vehicle for its rail journey, I reduced its weight considerably by removing much of the engine, the fuel tank, the gear box, the differential, and even the brake system. Without an engine to distribute brake fluid, there was really no point in having brakes, particularly given that the existing wheels were replaced with rail wheels, and the existing automotive braking system would have been useless. Luckily, the standard railroad gauge width of 1,435 mm was close enough to the vehicle's track width that new axles were not required. Given my new skills as a blacksmith, I was able to make the adaptation fairly easily. In effect, this version of the vehicle was no longer a car but rather a stainless steel shell, incapable of traveling under its own power—not unlike a stagecoach. A key modification was the installation of a color-coded temperature gauge so that Marty could have advance warning of the impending detonation of each presto log, which would be accompanied by a sudden burst of acceleration. The gauge also monitored the boiler temperature, giving us ample warning should it become so hot that the engine might explode.

RAIL WHEELS

THE RAIL WHEELS are actually standard 19th-century handcar wheels. The spokes were inverted to widen the stance and better match the distance between tracks.

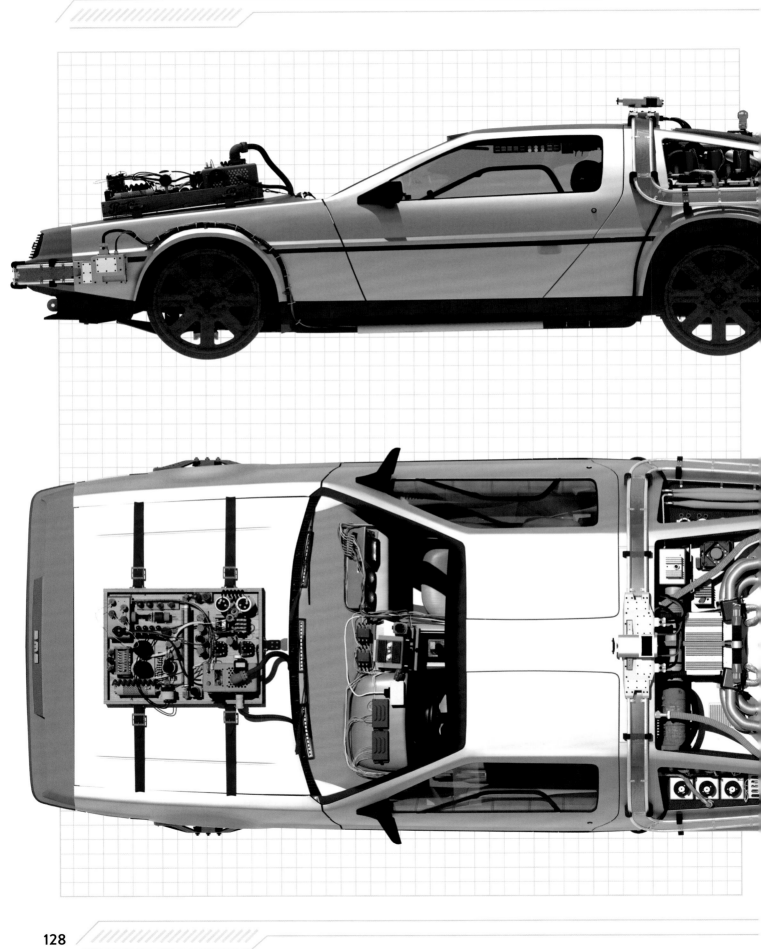

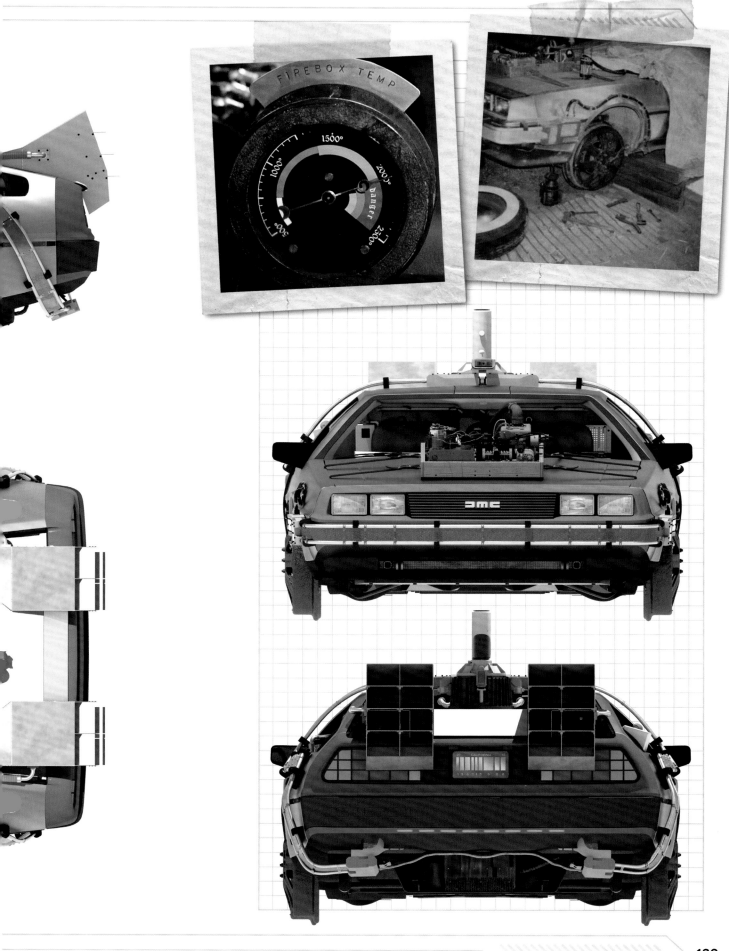

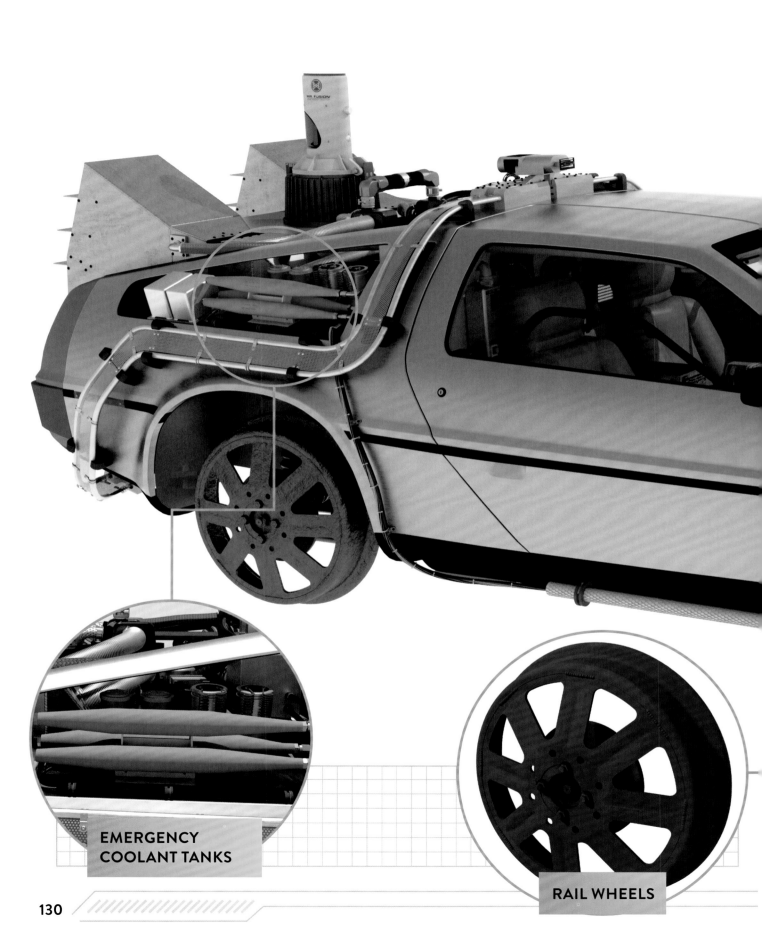

EMERGENCY
COOLANT TANKS

RAIL WHEELS

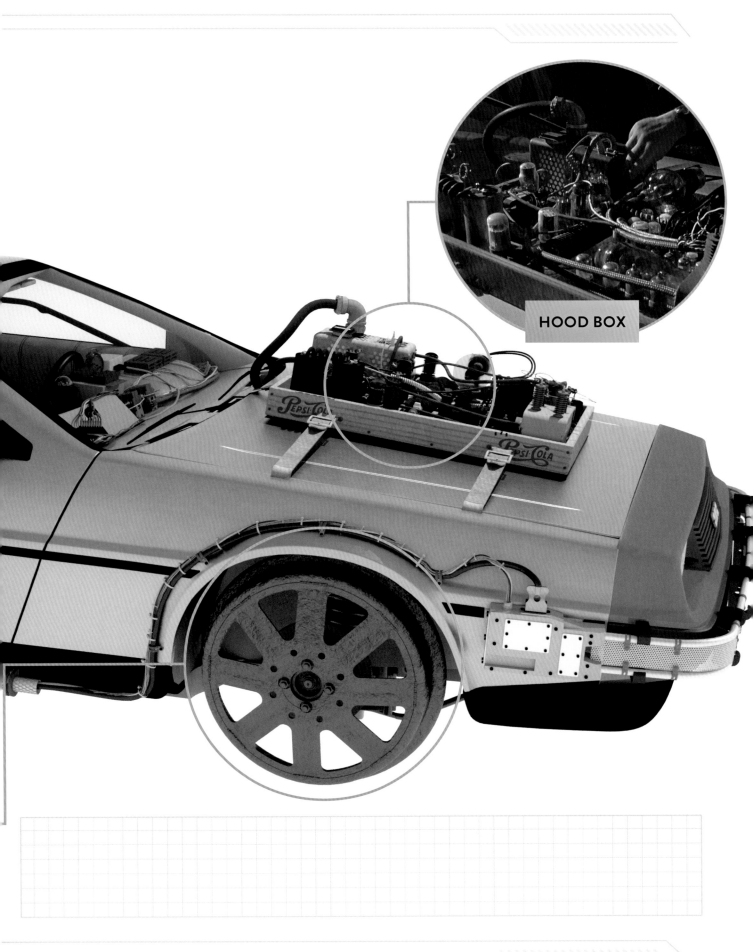

HOOD BOX

September 20, 1893

A detailed recounting of the construction of the Time Train is far too complex to relate here, because it involves the creation of a steam car time machine, a second DeLorean time vehicle, and visits to numerous eras to procure necessary components. I shall ultimately recount the full version in my memoirs. For now, I will provide an overview of the reason for its existence.

As a result of the theft of the time vehicle by old Biff Tannen in 2015 to provide his 1955 incarnation the means to become incredibly wealthy, young Biff turned Hill Valley into the dystopian "Hell Valley," a nightmarish alternate timeline that Marty and I corrected. After that experience, I vowed to be done with time travel and wished the destruction of the time vehicle. Days and weeks after the events of September 7, 1885, the day on which Marty returned to 1985, a recurring nightmare made me question that vow. Had Marty safely returned to 1985? If he did, I knew that he would take excellent care of Einstein, my faithful sheepdog, whom I'd left behind in my lab. But on several nights, I awakened in a cold sweat believing that upon arriving in 1985, Marty in the DeLorean was struck by an oncoming train in a head-on collision and completely obliterated. And if something had happened to Marty, what would become of poor Einstein, waiting patiently for human companionship in his little bed? I <u>had</u> to know.

And then there was Clara. Until I rescued schoolteacher Clara Clayton from a runaway buckboard, I had never believed in love at first sight. But upon meeting her, we were both struck by the proverbial thunderbolt. It was immediately clear we were soulmates, and we married on September 26. We shared all of our passions, secrets and dreams. Then, some months later, she sensed a malaise within me. Or perhaps I talked in my sleep. Regardless, she began asking me about time travel, my time machine, and my adventures in time. I was impressed at how quickly she grasped various concepts, and her ability to think "fourth dimensionally" exceeded Marty's. It was soon evident that nothing would make her happier than to be able to travel through time. She spoke about wanting to see the world I came from and even meeting my parents. The two of us spent many hours talking and daydreaming about trips we could take. To attend the premiere of a Beethoven symphony. To hear the Gettysburg Address. To visit the future. Thus the seeds were planted and had taken root. The conversations were no longer about "if," but "when." I would build a new time machine, confirm that Marty was safe, bring Einstein home with me, and explore the timestream, as I'd always intended.

The project would—and did—take time. Ironically, by knowing that time travel was a reality, the constraints of real time seemed less important. As far as Marty and Einstein were concerned, my traveling to October 27, 1985, from the year 1886 would be no different than traveling there from 1896. This fact relieved a tremendous amount of pressure—I was not racing against a ticking clock to complete my work, especially knowing that my health treatments in the future had added decades to my life. Eight years and two sons later, my dream would be realized, on September 9, 1893, when the Brown family embarked on our Time Train adventure...

TIME TRAIN AERIAL VIEW

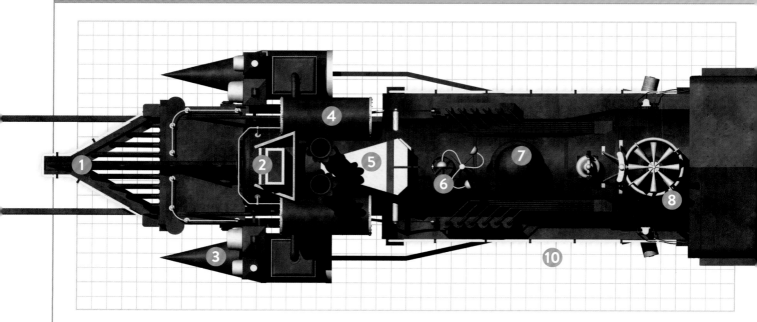

1. TIME LOOP KNIFE
2. FLUX CAPACITOR SYSTEM HOUSING
3. TEMPORAL FIELD AMPLIFIER
4. TEMPORAL SYSTEM CYLINDERS
5. COOLING INTAKE BELLOWS
6. PULSE-DOPPLER REGULATOR
7. STEAM DOME
8. TACHYON PULSE GENERATOR
9. CAB SKYLIGHT
10. FLUX BANDS
11. GENERATOR VENTS
12. REACTOR COOLING VENTS
13. MOLTEN FLUORIDE & THORIUM TUBE TO HEAT EXCHANGER
14. STEAM AND MSR RETURN
15. HEAT EXCHANGER

16 **REACTOR VESSEL, MOLTEN FLUORIDE SALT MIXED WITH THORIUM**

17 **REPROCESSING UNIT, 2 PUMPS AND 1 MIXER**

18 **STEAM TURBINES AND GENERATORS**

19 **REACTOR COOLING VENTS & RADIATION SCRUBBERS**

TENDER

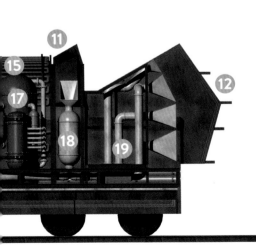

The Time Train Locomotive is a converted 4-6-0 locomotive, built by Rogers Locomotive and Machine Works. The eight-wheeled tender is custom-made for increased energy generation. Both cars are outfitted with flux bands to account for their movement during transit and because both cars need to travel safely through time together.

TIME TRAIN DETAILS

1. **TACHYON PULSE GENERATOR**
2. **STEAM DOME**
3. **GULL-WING CABIN DOOR**
4. **MAGNETIC FIELD CONTROL SYSTEM**
5. **FLUX FIELD REGULATOR**

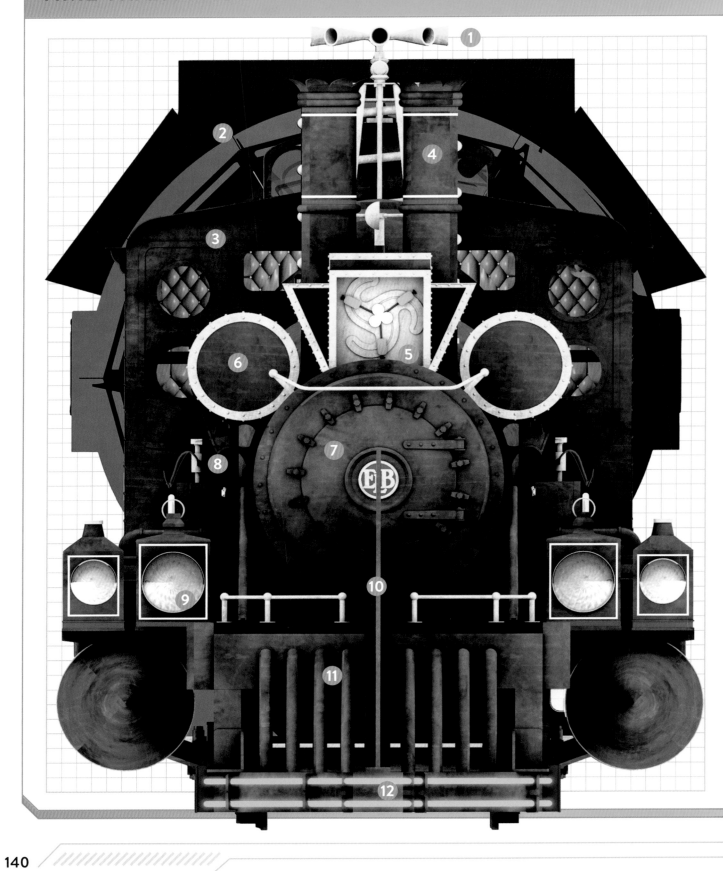

1. TEMPORAL FIELD AMPLIFIER
2. TENDER CONTAINING MSR REACTOR
3. LOCOMOTIVE CAB
4. SMOKESTACKS
5. FLUX CAPACITOR
6. TEMPORAL SYSTEM CYLINDERS
7. LOCOMOTIVE BOILER
8. ELECTRICAL SYSTEM DISTRIBUTOR
9. LIGHTS
10. TIME LOOP KNIFE
11. COWCATCHER
12. FLUX BANDS

LEFT: Concept sketch of the locomotive's flux capacitor. Its elements were ultimately revised so they could be constructed with parts more readily available in 1890.

TIME TRAIN CAB

1. ANALOG TIME DISPLAY
2. FLUX CAPACITOR OUTPUT GAUGE
3. TACHYON CHARGE GAUGE
4. TEMPORAL FIELD TACHYON REGULATOR
5. TACHYON INTAKE
6. REACTOR TEMPERATURE GAUGE
7. REACTOR PRESSURE GAUGE
8. BOILER TEMPERATURE GAUGE
9. SHIELDED "FIREBOX" REACTOR SYSTEMS
10. SPEEDOMETER
11. KOKEN BARBER PILOT SEAT
12. STEAM THROTTLE VALVE LEVER

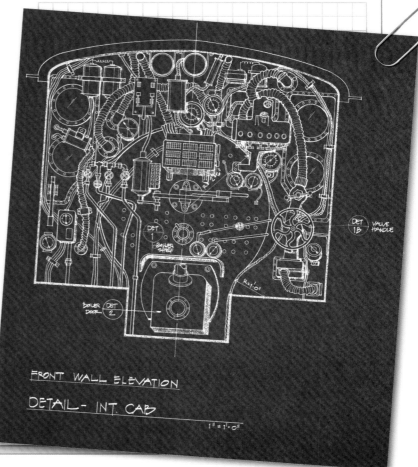

FRONT WALL ELEVATION

DETAIL - INT. CAB

1" = 1'-0"

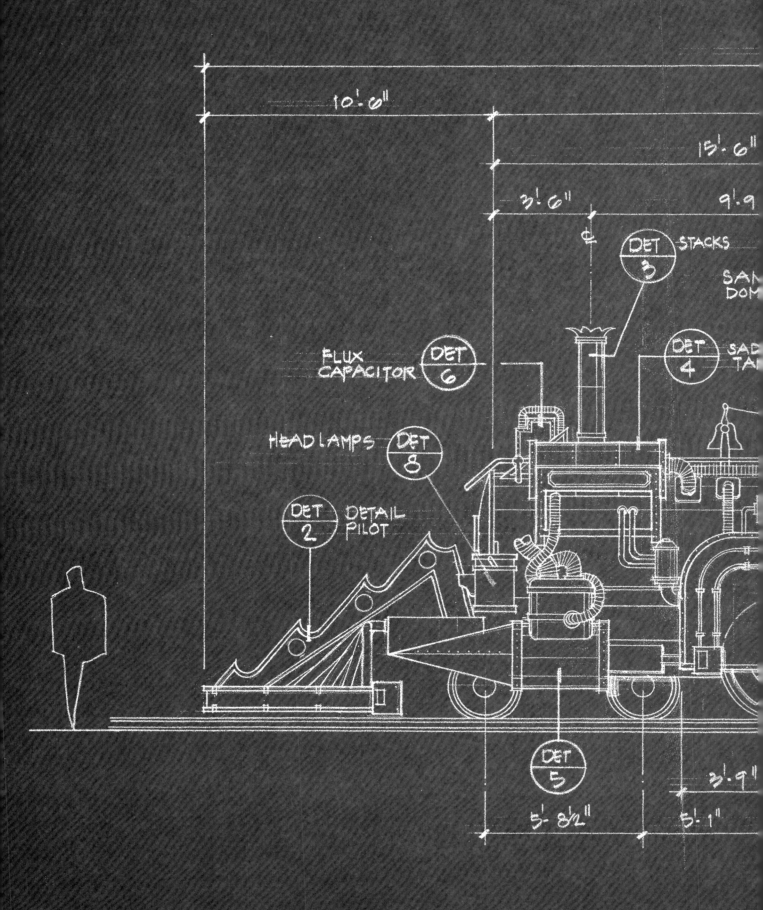

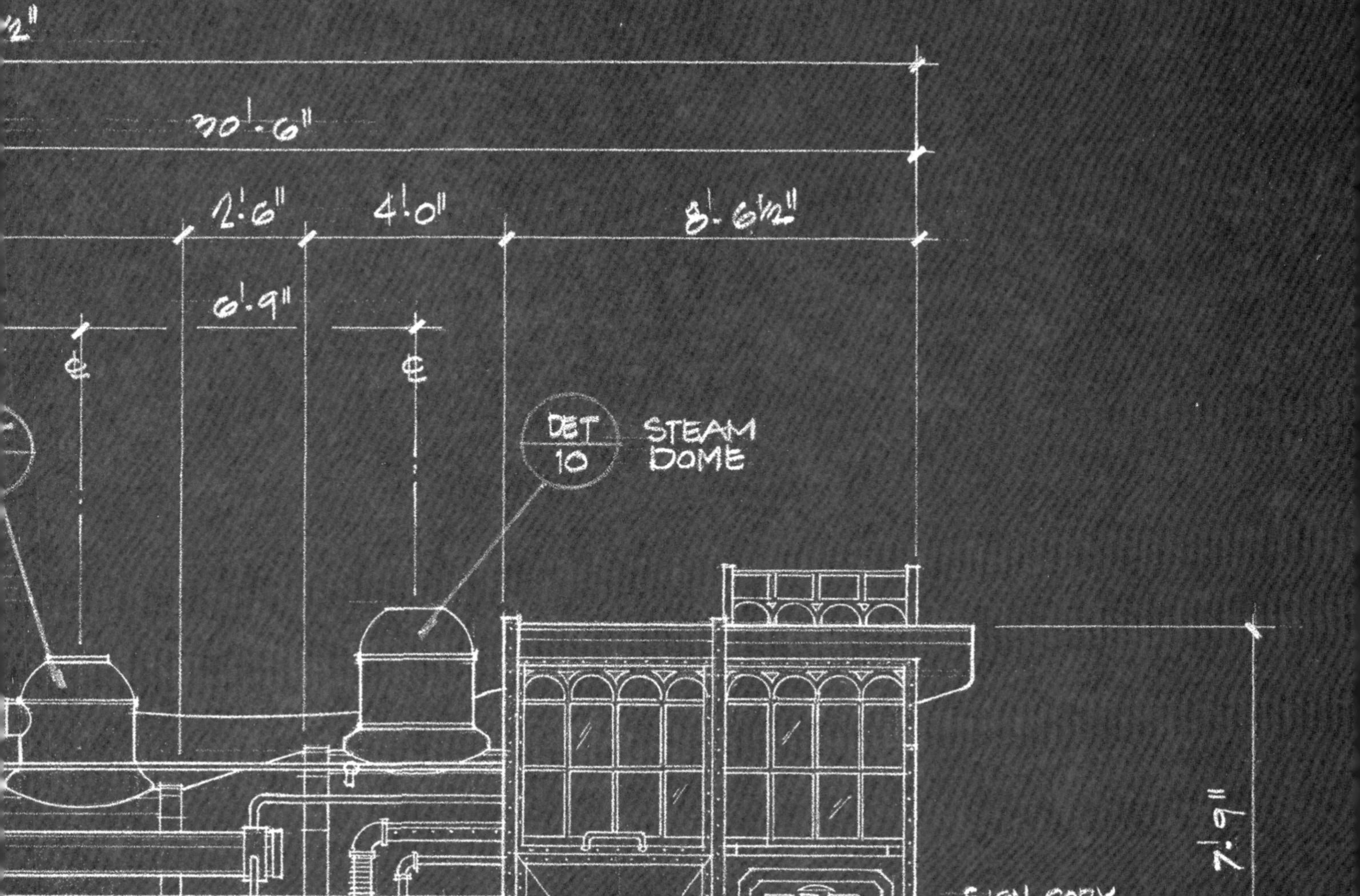

20'-6"

2'-6"   4'-0"   8'-6½"

6'-9"

DET
10   STEAM
DOME

ELB

SIGN COPY
AS DIR.

7'-9"

5'-0"

1'-9"

DET
13   WHEEL

3'-9"

5'-3"   8'-7"

BEHIND THE SCENES

WHY A DELOREAN?

The DeLorean was selected because it looked sexy, with the gull-wing doors giving it a unique, futuristic appearance (leading the Peabody family to mistake it for a "flying saucer" in the original *Back to the Future* film), and because of John DeLorean's notoriety—he was on trial while the movie was in preproduction, and the filmmakers thought this gave the car an added sense of danger.

HOW MANY CARS WERE USED?

For the original *Back to the Future* film, three stock DeLoreans were purchased, denoted as A, B, and C. The A car was the most detailed and best-looking car. It was used for all the close-ups and beauty shots. The B car was less detailed and was used for wide angle and driving shots. On the rare occasions when both the first and second units needed to film with a car, the B car was always relegated to the second unit. The C car was used for interior and process shots (see **Too Small for a Camera**, page 149).

For *Back to the Future Part II* and *Back to the Future Part III*, three more stock DeLoreans were acquired. Two of them were rebuilt as off-road vehicles, with more powerful engines and better suspension systems. The other was primarily used as the rail DeLorean seen in *Part III*, along with the A and B cars that also had train wheels installed. Additionally, a lightweight fiberglass replica was built for the wide angle flying car shots in *Part II* that required the actors to be seen inside the vehicle while airborne. This was achieved by use of a forklift or by suspending the replica with aircraft wire from a crane.

TOP: The fiberglass DeLorean could easily be moved around on a forklift. OPPOSITE TOP: A forklift was hidden behind the walls of the set so that the car could be lowered for its landing.

As of this writing, the meticulously restored A car is on display at the Petersen Automotive Museum in Los Angeles. The B car was destroyed by the locomotive at the end of *Part III*, and portions of the C car were used to create a replica for the Universal Studios Japan theme park that was subsequently auctioned off to a Japanese company. One of the off-road *Part III* cars is in private hands; it has been beautifully restored and makes appearances at conventions and *Back to the Future* events. The other off-road car rotted away and was combined with the remaining C car parts to create the vehicle used at the Japanese theme park. The rail DeLorean (along with the Time Train) was displayed at Universal's Florida theme park. Sadly, the fiberglass car deteriorated in storage and ultimately needed to be destroyed.

SPEEDOMETER

In the late 1970s, President Jimmy Carter mandated that speedometers in all cars sold in the United States should depict a maximum speed of 85 mph to discourage speeding. This directive applied to DeLoreans, but in the movie, the car needed to reach 88 mph in order to jump through time. Therefore, an overlay speedometer template that went to 95 mph was made. It was installed in the C car and used for all the shots of the analog speedometer.

⌐ DENTS

Prior to the advent of the DeLorean, one reason that stainless steel had never been used for a car body is that dents, no matter how small, could not be hammered out. A dented fender could not be repaired, only replaced, a situation that many DeLorean owners would come to lament. In the course of filming *Part III*, the demands of which put tremendous wear and tear on the cars, whenever a vehicle was dented, the body part was cannibalized from another production vehicle so that filming could continue.

THE GULL-WING DOOR STRUTS

Each gull-wing door is held open by a strut with a gas-filled cylinder, similar to those on screen doors. During filming of the *Back to the Future* scene on Town Square (shot on Universal's backlot) in which Doc instructs Marty about the lightning plan, the car door needed to remain open take after take. The outdoor temperature was near freezing, and during the takes, the gas in the strut's cylinder contracted, causing the door to slowly drop down and ruin the shot. To solve the issue, the special effects crew blasted the strut with hair dryers between takes, heating the gas inside, thereby making it possible to film for five minutes at a time.

TOO SMALL FOR A CAMERA

When shooting the original movie, the filmmakers were surprised to discover that the interior of the two-passenger DeLorean was too small for a 35mm Panaflex camera. There was simply no way to put the camera behind Marty McFly actor Michael J. Fox for any driving scenes, nor even to get a good side angle shot. Therefore, the C car was literally cut apart so that the camera could be placed in the desired places. All interior driving shots were filmed at Universal's Stage 12 using process photography by which the moving backgrounds were projected on a screen behind the vehicle.

TIME CIRCUITS DISPLAY

The months on the time circuits are shown as three-letter abbreviations instead of numbers to make it easier for the audience to understand and remember the dates. The filmmakers opted to use 12-hour time with a.m. and p.m. indicators instead of 24-hour time to make the displays consistent with the dialogue.

LEFT: Back of the C car showing the electronics needed to light the displays inside. BOTTOM: Robert Zemeckis directs Christopher Lloyd and Michael J. Fox in the C car gimbal rig, which was used to create the illusion of flying.

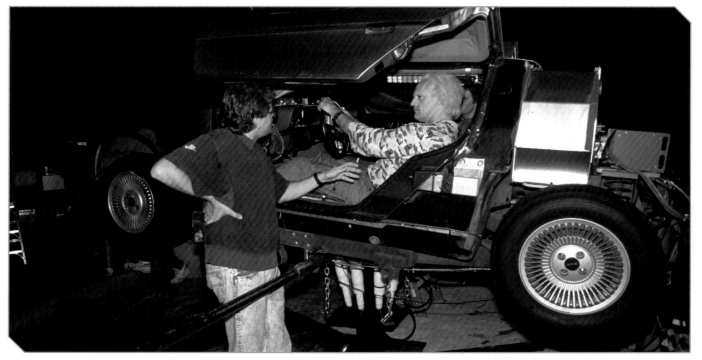

THE LICENSE PLATE

Whenever a license plate is featured in a movie or television show, the studio's legal department requires that it be approved by the particular state's Department of Motor Vehicles to ensure that it's not already in use. The filmmakers were unable to find a suitable seven-character plate, so they came up with the eight-character OUTATIME. All California plates had seven or fewer characters, so the OUTATIME plate did not need any legal approval because it was impossible for an eight-character plate to be in use.

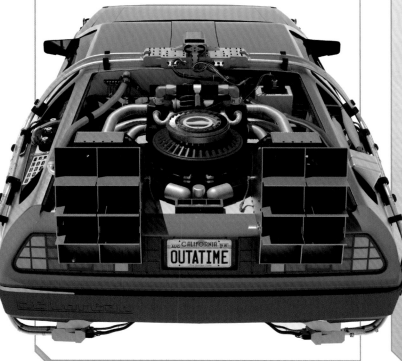

PRODUCT PLACEMENT

For the first film, Universal hired an outside product placement company to promote various products in the film in exchange for a fee to be split 50-50 with the production. One day, the head of the company came to producer Bob Gale to propose a deal worth $75,000, the equivalent of the cost of a day and half of shooting. All that was required was to change the DeLorean to a Ford Mustang. Incensed, Gale replied in no uncertain terms that "Doc Brown doesn't drive a @#$% Mustang." Some years later, Gale told the story at a DeLorean car show, and the next day, T-shirts were on sale featuring his quote.

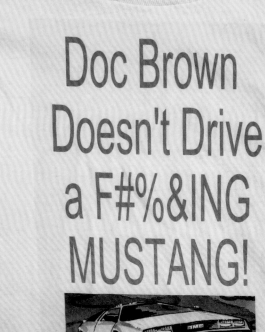

MINIATURES

Visual effects company ILM (Industrial Light & Magic) built two DeLorean miniatures over the course of the trilogy. The first was constructed for the flying car shot at the end of the original movie and was improved for use in *Part II*. The second was built for the train time-travel sequence in *Part III* in a larger scale. Two train miniatures were also built, one of the steam locomotive and one of the Time Train. The former was destroyed on camera in a "spectacular wreck," and the latter was used in the final shot in the trilogy.

WHY 88 MILES PER HOUR?

Over the years, many theories have been proposed about the significance of 88 mph—the speed at which time travel occurs in *Back to the Future*. Fans have often speculated that it represents the character for infinity (∞) duplicated sideways. But the real reason is far simpler: The film's creators felt 88 mph was easy to remember and significantly higher than the legal speed limit, meaning Doc Brown wouldn't accidentally drive that fast!

DELOREAN TIME MACHINE CONCEPT ART

IN AUGUST 1984, production illustrator Andrew Probert joined the *Back to the Future* production to draw storyboards for the Twin Pines mall sequence and an ultimately abandoned nuclear test site sequence (replaced by the clock tower sequence in the final film). Probert also began conceptualizing the DeLorean Time Machine. By the end of August, the filmmakers decided that Probert's designs were too slick and did not reflect the idea that Doc Brown had modified a DeLorean in his garage. Artist Ron Cobb, whom Zemeckis and Gale had met a few years earlier and whose art had an "earthier" style, was hired in September to solve the conundrum. Cobb came up with an inner logic to the nuclear reactor, making it flush with the vehicle and added a single cooling vent. He also came up with what are now called the flux bands and designed the interior of the vehicle. The filmmakers were pleased with his work and had Probert refine the designs by reconfiguring the flux bands, adding a second cooling vent, and reworking the interior. Probert's drawings were then used by car designer Michael Scheffe, who was tasked with realizing the vehicle's final design.

SIDE VIEWS

8/20 The key feature is the huge nuclear reactor.

8/21 The nuclear reactor has been redesigned and an exterior conduit added along the sides.

8/23 Improving on the previous version, this one has a reconfigured conduit.

8/28 Wheel covers added and all the rear components exposed.

8/29 Front view of the 8/28 version.

ROBERT 082984

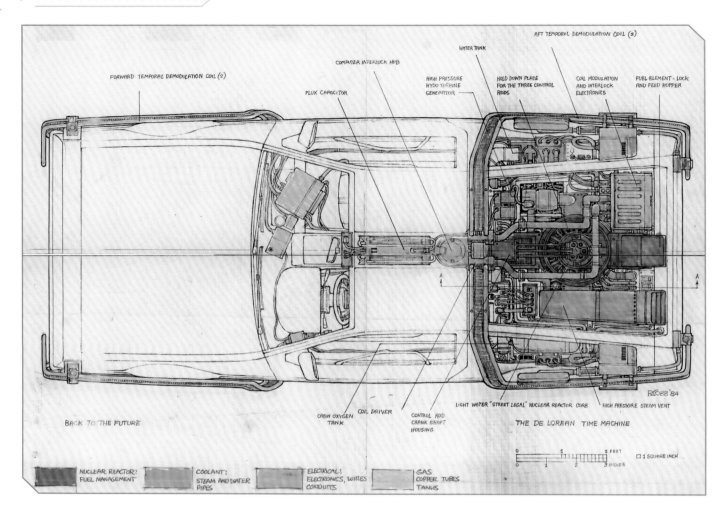

FORWARD TEMPORAL DEMODULATION COIL (2)

COMPUTER INTERLOCK HUB

FLUX CAPACITOR

WATER TANK

AFT TEMPORAL DEMODULATION COIL (2)

HIGH PRESSURE HYDRO TURBINE GENERATOR

HOLD DOWN PLATE FOR THE THREE CONTROL RODS

COIL MODULATION AND INTERLOCK ELECTRONICS

FUEL ELEMENT - LOCK AND FEED HOPPER

CABIN OXYGEN TANK

COIL DRIVER

CONTROL ROD CRANK SHAFT HOUSING

LIGHT WATER "STREET LEGAL" NUCLEAR REACTOR CORE

HIGH PRESSURE STEAM VENT

RCOBB '84

BACK TO THE FUTURE

THE DE LOREAN TIME MACHINE

NUCLEAR REACTOR: FUEL MANAGEMENT

COOLANT: STEAM AND WATER PIPES

ELECTRICAL: ELECTRONICS, WIRES CONDUITS

GAS COPPER TUBES TANKS

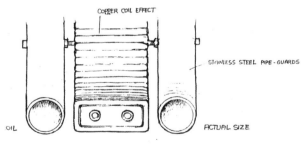

COPPER COIL EFFECT

STAINLESS STEEL PIPE-GUARDS

OIL

ACTUAL SIZE

(Overhead Schematics) Cobb came up with names for key components. His color-coded version breaks down the different systems by function. The "hub cap" design for the central reactor element was incorporated in the final design.

(Front and Back views) Cobb added coils (flux bands) visible in front and back views of the vehicle as well as a single cooling vent.

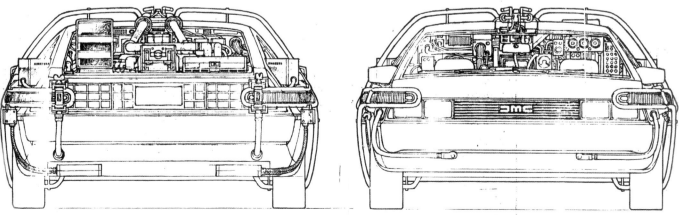

COCKPIT INTERIOR

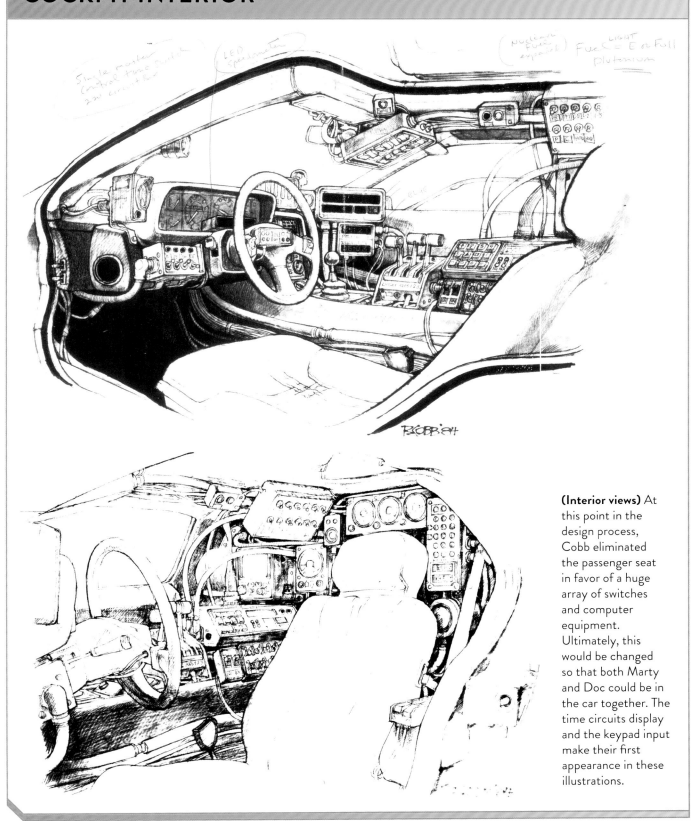

(Interior views) At this point in the design process, Cobb eliminated the passenger seat in favor of a huge array of switches and computer equipment. Ultimately, this would be changed so that both Marty and Doc could be in the car together. The time circuits display and the keypad input make their first appearance in these illustrations.

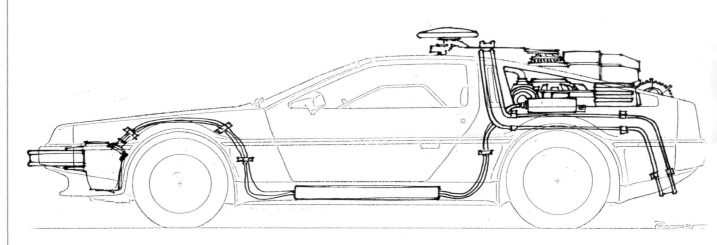

10/10 Side view without the cooling vents and featuring an earlier reactor design. The coils and cabling are now in their final configuration.

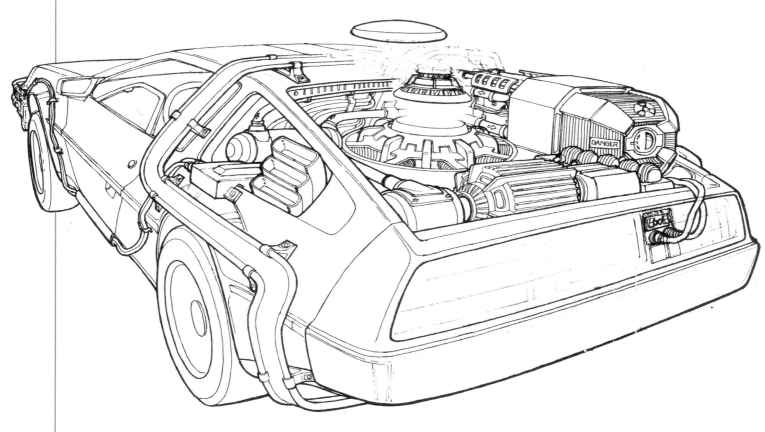

10/10 Rear view version of the above. The reactor elements are too big, and there are no cooling vents.

Probert 101184

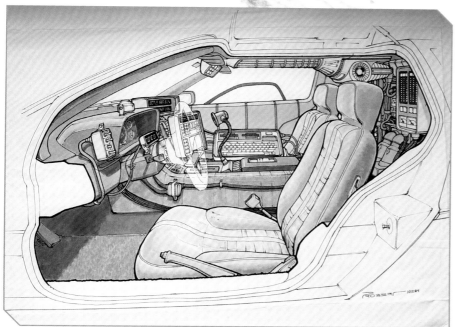

Probert 101284

10/11 Rear final. The October 11 drawings are Probert's final versions. The reactor has been lowered, the vents are in their final configuration, and the license plate reads TIMELESS.

10/12 Interior. In this concept, the passenger seat has been restored and the time circuits display has begun to look closer to those seen in the final film. A digital speedometer has also been added to the steering column. The full computer keyboard was deemed unnecessary, however, and a telephone-style keypad was ultimately used as an input device.

THE ENDURING POPULARITY OF THE DELOREAN TIME MACHINE

IN POLLS AND SURVEYS taken by the *UK Telegraph*, *Classic Cars Journal*, *Esquire*, and other sources, the DeLorean Time Machine regularly ranks at or near the top position as the number-one movie car of all time. Perhaps a contributing factor to this perennial popularity is that, unlike the Batmobile and James Bond's cars—which regularly changed (sometimes radically) over the life of these franchises—the DeLorean Time Machine has remained consistent and easily identifiable throughout the trilogy, as well as in the subsequent animated series and comic books. The DeLorean's popularity is reflected in the huge number of time vehicle toys, models, and paraphernalia that have been produced throughout the years, including over a 100 scale replicas ranging in size from 1:6 to 1:87, and even smaller key-chain versions.

Some *Back to the Future* fans are content to collect toys, posters, and other movie memorabilia, but others take their devotion a step further, by purchasing a DeLorean automobile. And many of those car owners go the ultimate distance, by modifying their vehicles into Time Machine replicas. For those who aren't adept technically or who lack patience, there are professional car customizers who can do the work for them. But regardless of whether they've done a "BTTF mod," the majority of DeLorean owners have their vehicle because of *Back to the Future*. The timeless beauty of the vehicle turns heads wherever it goes, especially whenever its gull-wing doors are opened.

In May 2015, in honor of the 30th anniversary of the first film, the major annual automobile event Las Vegas Car Stars featured a salute to the DeLorean,

BELOW: DeLorean Time Machine collectibles.

TOP: Twenty-seven DeLoreans prepare to parade down the Las Vegas Strip, May 2015. ABOVE: The convention floor at the 2016 DeLorean Convention and Show, Springfield, Illinois.

attended by many of the movie's cast. The highlight was a DeLorean parade down Las Vegas Boulevard, with 27 DeLoreans all driving with both doors open, carrying Christopher Lloyd (Doc Brown), Lea Thompson (Lorraine McFly), and other cast and crew. Seven of the vehicles were *Back to the Future* modified, making this the largest group of DeLorean Time Machines ever in one place.

There are DeLorean Owner Associations all over the world, and their members regularly get together for events in various locations. The biannual DCS (DeLorean Convention and Show) takes place every other summer in a different US locale. Owners show off their vehicles, swap tips and stories, attend talks and seminars, shop for aftermarket parts, and participate in organized group drives. There are always a few

Time Machines on display, along with other uniquely modified vehicles. Some have speculated that had *Back to the Future* been released in 1981 while vehicles were still coming off the assembly line, the DeLorean Motor Company might have remained in business. That is an alternate timeline that only Doc Brown could explore. However, it's safe to say that in our own timeline, the DeLorean Time Machine will continue to delight audiences throughout the world for decades to come.

Originally published in the US by Insight Editions, San Rafael, California, in 2021.
This UK edition first published by Haynes Publishing in April 2021.
Reprinted August 2024

A catalogue record for this book is available from the British Library.

ISBN: 9781785217333

Published by Haynes Group Ltd
Sparkford, Yeovil, Somerset, BA22 7JJ, UK
Website: www.haynes.com

Publisher: Raoul Goff
Associate Publisher: Vanessa Lopez
Creative Director: Chrissy Kwasnik
Designers: Judy Wiatrek Trum and Amazing15
Executive Editor: Chris Prince
Editorial Assistant: Anna Wostenberg
Managing Editor: Lauren LePera
Senior Production Editor: Elaine Ou
VP of Manufacturing: Alix Nicholaeff
Production Associate: Eden Orlesky
Senior Production Manager: Greg Steffen

Cutaway hoverboard illustration by Ian Moores
Unit photography by Ralph Nelson
Original *Back to the Future Part II* hoverboard concept art by John Bell
Original *Back to the Future Part III* 1885 concept art by Marty Kline
Additional concept art by Michael Scheffe and Simon Wells

Special thanks to Jay Kogan, Liam Bogan, and Tatum Galliete at DC Entertainment, Stephen Clark, Steve Concotelli, John Barber, IDW Publishing, and the DeLorean Motor Company.

Manufactured in China by Insight Editions

ACKNOWLEDGMENTS

Joe Walser led the team that restored the original A car DeLorean Time Machine (on display at the Petersen Automotive Museum in LA), and has built several replicas on his own. Being so intimately familiar with every nuance of the vehicle, he was the only person who could co-author this book. His perfectionism, incredible focus, and hard work made it truly definitive. No one else could have done what he did, and for that, I am immensely grateful. Thanks, Joe, times a googolplex! My equal thanks to editor Chris Prince, who put up with more than he might have expected to get this book to print. His commitment to quality is clear on every page, and he never failed to keep his eyes on the prize. A special shout-out to John Barber at IDW Publishing, who contributed to Doc Brown's backstory. And to everyone else involved, 1.21 giga-thanks to all of you, both at Insight and especially to everyone acknowledged by Joe.
—Bob Gale

Additional Logical Systems Deconstruction and Nomenclature: Steve Concotelli, Tycho Wijnans, Terry Matalas, and Scott Miller with contributions by Chad Schweitzer, Jerry Holbrook, Tom Silknitter, and the DeLorean Time Machine community.

The 3D DeLorean Time Machine model created for this book contains over 20,000 individual elements, effectively a complete digital version of the 2013 museum quality restoration of the DeLorean Time Machine used in all three *Back to the Future* movies.

3D modeling team: Art Director, Joe Walser. Lead Modelers, Tycho Wijnans and Scott Miller. Modelers: Mark Dehlinger, Ed Hillery, Tim Whiteman, Antonio Drabble, and Rob Depew. Additional Modelers: Charles Kline, Nathan Clark, Gary Higginbotham, Corrie Hollingsworth, Gareth Williams, Spencer Boyle, Clifford James Boyle, Gary Nagle, and Steven Dodds.

Other contributions: Sean Bishop; Rob Klein; Chad Schweitzer; Eddie Dennis; Joe Kovacs; Mike "Crash" Wolterbeek; Ken Kapalowski; Ara Kourchians; Alex Abdalla; Andrew Wells; Jerry Holbrook; Stephen Clark; Michael Klastorin; Elliot Hansen; Cindy Walser; Jessica, Joey, Jacob, and Jackson Walser; Diane Miller; and Marci Concotelli.

Special thanks to @Ted7, and @Petersen Automotive Museum for the use of their spectacular photos; to Andrew Probert and the late Ron Cobb for their stunning visual contributions; to Kevin Pike, Michael Scheffe, and their creative team who made the DeLorean Time Machine real; to Michael Lantieri and company who built the Time Train and sequel cars; to Universal Studios; and to Bob Gale and Robert Zemeckis, without whom none of this would have been possible.
—Joe Walser